I0411469

United States
Department
of Agriculture

Forest Service

Rocky Mountain
Research Station

General Technical Report
RMRS-GTR-309

September 2013

Review and Recommendations for Climate Change Vulnerability Assessment Approaches With Examples From the Southwest

Megan M. Friggens, Karen E. Bagne, Deborah M. Finch,
Donald Falk, Jack Triepke, Ann Lynch

Friggens, M.; Bagne, K.; Finch, D.; Falk, D.; Triepke, J.; Lynch, A. 2013. **Review and recommendations for climate change vulnerability assessment approaches with examples from the Southwest.** Gen. Tech. Rep. RMRS-GTR-309. Fort Collins, CO: U.S. Department of Agriculture, Forest Service, Rocky Mountain Research Station. 106 p.

ABSTRACT

Climate change creates new challenges for resource managers and decision-makers with broad and often complex effects that make it difficult to accurately predict and design management actions to minimize undesirable impacts. We review pertinent information regarding methods and approaches used to conduct climate change vulnerability assessments to reveal assumptions and appropriate application of results. Secondly, we provide managers with an updated summary of knowledge regarding vulnerability of species and habitats to climate change in the American Southwest. Overall, vulnerability assessments provided valuable information on climate change effects and possible management actions but were far from a comprehensive picture for the future of the Southwest. Scales, targets, and assessment approaches varied widely and focused on only a subset of resources. We recommend land managers critically examine methods when using assessment results; select scale, methods, and targets carefully when planning new assessments; and communicate assessment needs to researchers of climate change response.

Keywords: Resource management, wildlife, wildlands, conservation, global change

AUTHORS

Megan Friggens is a Research Ecologist with the U.S. Department of Agriculture, Forest Service, Rocky Mountain Research Station.

Karen Bagne is an Ecologist and Wildlife Biologist with the USDA Forest Service, Rocky Mountain Research Station.

Deborah Finch is the Program Manager for the Grassland, Shrubland, and Desert program of the USDA Forest Service, Rocky Mountain Research Station.

Donald Falk is Associate Professor in the University of Arizona School of Natural Resources and the Environment, with joint appointments in the Laboratory of Tree-Ring Research and Institute of the Environment.

Jack Triepke is a Regional Ecologist for the USDA Forest Service Southwestern Region in Albuquerque, New Mexico. Jack is also a Ph.D. candidate at the University of New Mexico where he is studying the effects of climate change on Southwest ecosystems.

Ann Lynch is a Research Entomologist with the Rocky Mountain Research Station, stationed in Tucson, AZ.

ACKNOWLEDGMENTS

Funding for this project was provided by the Western Wildlands Environmental Threats Assessment Center. We thank Aimee Roberson and Cathryn Dowd whose comments improved this manuscript.

Cover photo: Sevilleta National Wildlife Refuge LTER Grassland (photo by Megan Friggens); hurricane Ileana approaches the Baja Peninsula August 24, 2006 (NASA-Goddard Space Flight Center, data from NOAA GOES); Waldo Canyon burn scar (brown) outside of Colorado Springs, Colorado, 2012 (NASA).

EXECUTIVE SUMMARY

The intent of this report is, first, to review pertinent information regarding methods and approaches used to conduct climate change vulnerability assessments and, second, to provide managers with an updated summary of knowledge regarding vulnerability to climate change of species and habitats in the American Southwest. We begin by defining and discussing climate change vulnerability assessment concepts and approaches and then examine major methods by which such assessments are conducted. Finally, we review and synthesize the information presented in vulnerability assessments conducted for the southwestern United States.

Climate change creates new challenges for resource managers and decision-makers, with broad and often complex effects that make it difficult to design management actions that can minimize undesirable impacts. A wide range of approaches have been used to predict how and why resources will change in response to climate change. Assessments can be useful in addressing climate change issues because they synthesize large amounts of complex information. Vulnerability assessments seek to synthesize available information on climate change for a region, sector, or resource of interest and glean recommendations for management actions. Vulnerability is a combination of exposure, sensitivity, and adaptive capacity, components that are not always distinct nor are they integrated into every vulnerability assessment (USGCRP 2011). By specifically examining vulnerability to climate change, managers can rank needs as well as pinpoint the causes of vulnerability for valued resources. Most vulnerability assessments fit one of four broad categories: mathematical models, conceptual frameworks, indices, and syntheses.

A number of important elements must be considered when preparing to conduct a vulnerability assessment, including selecting targets, scales, and the measure of vulnerability. Vulnerability assessments that address questions that managers and stakeholders can act upon are more applicable than assessments that lack immediate relevance to on-the-ground actions. Depending upon the objective, identified assessment targets may include individuals, populations, species, landscapes, and ecosystem processes. Selection of appropriate biological, spatial, and temporal scales influences the relevance of biological analysis in any assessment of climate change vulnerability. Assessments also need to integrate considerations of critical thresholds and important ecosystem tipping points. Modeling and empirical studies suggest that changes due to climate alone are likely to be expressed at multi-annual to decadal time scales (Allen and Breshears 1998). In contrast, severe large-scale disturbances can reorganize mass and energy of ecosystems on much shorter time scales of days to months (Overpeck and others 1990). In some scenarios, combinations of gradual climate change and disturbance events will trigger abrupt ecosystem transitions into novel configurations, rather than either factor acting alone.

Methods for measuring climate change response are organized into four groups: hydrologic models, adaptive capacity models, distribution models, and indices. Hydrologic models are a critical component of assessments based within aquatic systems and often inform other modeling approaches aimed at species or biomes. Hydrologic models encompass a variety of mostly statistical approaches that estimate the impact of climate change on hydrological function and aquatic systems and can incorporate both ecological and economic aspects of system vulnerability. Various approaches, grouped together in this report in the Adaptive Capacity Models section, identify individual characteristics that may influence the capacity of species to survive changes to climate. Although diverse, adaptive capacity models include estimates of species survival (or, alternatively, risk of extinction) as well as mechanisms of local adaptation (for example, latent genetic variation that may confer resistance to emerging climate conditions). Distribution models, the most commonly used method to predict response, encompass a variety of statistical, simulation, and other approaches to estimate future effects of climate on the range distributions of species, communities, and biomes. These models may generate predictions of future habitat suitability for species or communities, habitat characteristics, or patterns of biodiversity. Finally, a variety of methods aim to prioritize the identification and management of species or habitats. Our discussion focuses on a subset of these methods, termed indices or index-based measures that identify relative vulnerability within a group of targeted study subjects through a quantitative comparison of traits or issues. Index-based measures have emerged within the literature only recently in response to limitations in directly measuring climate change response.

A vulnerability assessment examines the expected response of resources, how the resource becomes more or less in need of management, especially in relation to other resources or a critical level, and identifies management intervention points. A vulnerability assessment is a specific type of product that identifies how current management strategies may change under changing climate by combining information on the expected response of individual resources with information on how such impacts change relative management needs among multiple resources. Thus, vulnerability is often measured in relation to a reference level that is relevant to contemporary human societies. The specific measure of vulnerability used in an assessment is important to understanding the conclusions and possible limitations of the assessment. Six common measures of vulnerability to climate change are used in natural resource management:

(1) Direct observations of response to recent versus historic conditions.

(2) Departure of modeled future of climate, species distributions, biodiversity, and other measures from baseline observations.

(3) Observations from experiments or of past events equivalent to projected future conditions.

(4) Proximity to thresholds or probability of exceeding a critical threshold.

(5) Estimates of adaptive capacity to future conditions.

(6) Relative importance of modeled factors affecting response.

Projections for the United States indicate that the Southwest is likely to experience more extreme climate changes than other regions. These changes exacerbate existing problems associated with sustaining valued natural resources. For example, longer duration droughts and higher temperatures will tax the already scarce water sources critical to plants, fish, and wildlife as well as to the rapidly expanding human population that occupies the Southwest. For these reasons, we focus our review of climate change vulnerability assessments on those applicable to natural resource management in the Southwest. Several common themes are found among these assessments:

- Vulnerability of grasslands to invasive species is likely to increase under climate change (reviews by Morgan and others 2010; Chambers and Pellant 2008; Neilson and others 2010)
- Hydrological systems will be taxed by multiple impacts, including:
  o higher water temperatures with multiple effects for temperature dependent species (Johnson and others 2005; Eaton and Scheller 1996).
  o changes in precipitation events leading to less snowpack, changes to the timing of flood regimes, less flow, and reduced water tables (Theobald and others 2009).
  o spread of invasive species in both aquatic and riparian habitats (Theobald and others 2009; Rood and Conrad 2008).
- Many studies show that temperature alone drives or is sufficient to lead to observed or predicted changes (see Williams and others 2010 for tree growth; Currie 2001 for biodiversity; Garfin and Lenart 2007 for loss of cool water fish species; Notaro and others 2012; Williams and others 2012 trees; Eaton and Scheller 1996 and Meyers and others 1999 describe many effects on aquatic systems,) but note exception to temperature-driven patterns for cheatgrass invasion (see Bradley 2009).
- Areas near ecotones are more vulnerable to change (e.g., Madrean habitats see Kupfer and others 2005).

Overall, vulnerability assessments reviewed in this synthesis provided valuable information on climate change effects and possible management actions, but were unable to provide a comprehensive picture for the future of the Southwest. Scales, targets, and assessment approaches varied widely and focused on only a subset of resources. Assessments of animal species typically involved special status species and were primarily assessed using index-based approaches though reports from these assessments provide detailed information on sources and causes of species vulnerability. Community level assessments varied more and included statistical modeling methods. Plant assessments tended to cover a wider geographic range than those focused on animals. Distribution models were used more widely for plant species and functional groups but were biased towards forested ecosystems. From many of these assessments, researchers are able to provide spatially explicit estimates of future climate and habitat suitability for animal and plant species. The applicability of vulnerability assessments for the Southwest is limited by the degree to which they include accurate measures of future change. Measuring future vulnerability was difficult where projected climate change impacts in the region exceed historical events, emphasizing the need for process-based models and the inclusion of critical thresholds. In addition, there were few assessments that integrate multiple complex interactions and threats such as those posed by disease, pests, invasive species, and hydrological changes. These gaps are likely mirrored for assessments in other regions. We recommend land managers critically examine methods when using assessment results; select scale, methods, and targets carefully when planning new assessments; and communicate assessment needs to researchers of climate change response.

CONTENTS

Tables

Figures

Chapter 1. Vulnerability Assessments in Natural Resource Management: Overview and Application

1.1 The Climate Change Challenge

The impacts of climate change on global ecosystems are apparent, and future change is likely to be dramatic (Nicholls Cazenave 2010; Williams and others 2010; Chen and others 2011; Notaro and others 2012). Climate change is emerging as a dominant challenge for resource managers and decision-makers. The breadth and complexity of climate change effects make it difficult to accurately detect, predict or understand the full range of impacts on ecosystems and, therefore, to design management actions that can minimize undesirable effects. Management based only on current or recent past conditions may not be adequate to address long-term changes in resources prompted by climate change (Millar and others 2007). Consequently, it is critical to plan ahead based on evidence and predictions of future climate and related impacts. Climate change vulnerability assessments seek to synthesize the available information on changes of and responses to climate for a region, sector, or resource of interest. Through this synthesis, assessments can be used to identify priority and effective management options that are essential considering the limitations of time, money, and personnel. The need for assessments accompanied by proactive and targeted management is great because a large number of stressors affect natural and human systems, the pace of environmental change is rapid, and management resources are limited. Vulnerability assessments cover a wide range of topics, methods, and scales. In this report, we outline key concepts, assessment methods, modeling approaches, and provide guidance for using assessments for natural resource management under climate change.

1.2 Climate Change Vulnerability Assessments

The Intergovernmental Panel on Climate Change (IPCC) defines vulnerability to climate change as "the degree to which a system is susceptible to, and unable to cope with, adverse effects of climate change, including climate variability and extremes" (Solomon and others 2007). Vulnerability assessments are a fundamental tool available to many disciplines and sectors but are particularly applicable to management of natural resources, which is the focus of this document. Vulnerability is a combination of exposure, sensitivity, and adaptive capacity, although these components are not always distinct nor are all three always integrated into every vulnerability assessment (USGCRP 2011; Fig. 1.1). Essentially, the response of a system, species, or individual to climate change will depend on: (1) the effects to which it is exposed, (2) how it responds to or is sensitive to those impacts, and (3) its capacity to ameliorate the effects it experiences. Vulnerability assessments generally differ from impact assessments, which identify and quantify the effects of climate change, by focusing on the causes of and variation in expected impacts with the specific intent to identify effective and efficient management actions that will reduce the negative impacts predicted (Füssel and Klein 2005; Glick and others 2011). Another approach similar to a vulnerability assessment is a risk assessment or decision analysis, which focuses on the probability of negative outcomes and their consequences. The negative outcome is a set impact threshold, and

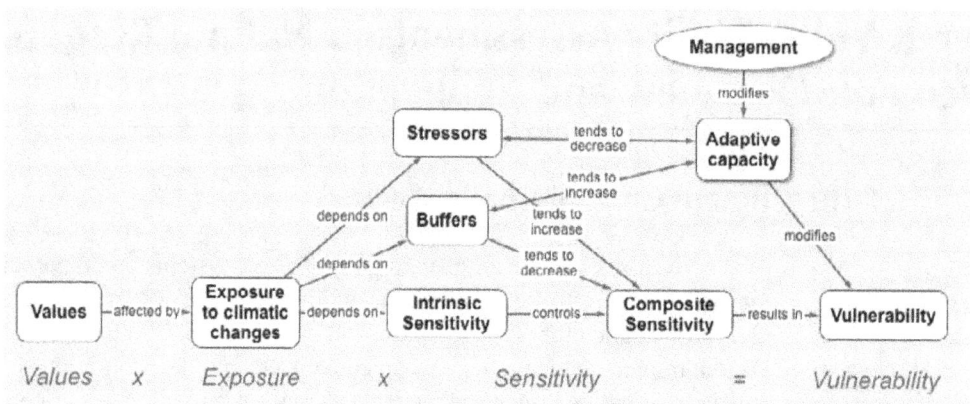

Figure 1.1. Conceptual model for assessing vulnerability, showing linkages among exposure, values, and system condition (sensitivity). The authors distinguish three components of sensitivity for their systems. "Buffers" and "stressors" are human-induced, whereas "intrinsic sensitivity" is based on inherent characteristics independent of human influence (Furniss and others 2012: Fig. 2). This diagram demonstrates the relationship between management and vulnerability.

a risk assessment can directly incorporate the uncertainty surrounding predicted impacts (Harwood 2000; Jones 2001). If only the probability of negative outcomes are assessed, a risk assessment is essentially a vulnerability assessment, but often these risk-focused approaches take further steps to incorporate decision analysis, which can weigh the effect of different management options on the outcome and estimate the accompanying uncertainty (Harwood 2000).

Climate change issues are well addressed by vulnerability assessments, which can synthesize large amounts of complex information. By examining vulnerability to climate change, managers can rank needs as well as pinpoint the causes of vulnerability for valued resources. Assessing vulnerability can also identify species and systems that are resilient or even have a positive response to climate change, such as future increases in range or local abundance (Notaro and others 2012; Quijada-Mascaranas and others, submitted). Resources with predicted positive responses may also need to be managed if their responses negatively affect vulnerable or priority resources. Some highly vulnerable subjects may be low priority if no effective actions to reduce vulnerability can be taken, if the cost of action is excessive, or if the subject is deemed of less immediate value than other targets. In developing management strategies, managers will need to consider vulnerability to multiple disturbances, including climate change, in relation to other prioritization factors such as policy, feasibility, and economics.

Once practitioners have gathered and processed information on climate change impacts and vulnerabilities for their selected targets, the next step is to use that information to decide if actions are needed and to design those actions to be most effective and efficient. Applying vulnerability measures helps reduce complex information and identify expected impacts. However, vulnerability assessments are not the only tools for determining management actions. For example, management priorities and target sensitivities may already be known or set by other priorities unrelated to vulnerability. Multiple targets can be integrated into a single vulnerability assessment so that susceptibilities of multiple areas can be combined. These integrated assessments, however, are less common and require that some relationship among the targets be defined. Spatial approaches are conducive to assessing multiple sectors simultaneously, but not all targets of interest can always be represented spatially.

1.3 Vulnerability Assessment Approaches

A wide range of approaches has been used to assess natural resources impacted by climate change and to glean management recommendations. Mathematical modeling approaches to estimate change or probability of change are common and can range from complex sets of equations representing multiple influencing factors or aspects of the resource to indices that distill response into ranks or classification representing vulnerability. Mathematical modeling covers a large number of methods, which are outlined in Table 3.1 and detailed in Appendix 1. All models are limited in their ability to represent all contributing processes and factors. Indices simplify response and are specifically designed to address vulnerability and transition easily to management recommendations. More complex models focus on improving predicted response, but their results often need to be translated into a measure of vulnerability (see Chapter 4). Conceptual frameworks focus on the relationships and linkages among factors, resource targets, and interacting elements. Conceptual frameworks can be used to clarify goals or identify key elements and are often used when vulnerability is assessed through a consensus of experts or stakeholders (Table 3.2). Frameworks are well suited to incorporating local issues and, like indices, can be effective even when information is sparse. Synthesis is a common assessment approach that collects available information on impacts and the resource of interest to compile knowledge and glean recommendations. Included information may be derived from any number of approaches, including modeling, experimental studies, or expert opinion. Because a synthesis gathers, reviews, and integrates information, there is no specific methodology for ranking or formally integrating information sources, but a large number of disparate aspects can be combined and factors other than vulnerability can be included (e.g., legal requirements, costs, and cultural values). Note that these approaches are not mutually exclusive and a single assessment may integrate multiple approaches.

1.4 Steps for Conducting a Vulnerability Assessment

Climate change vulnerability assessments are a mechanism for natural resource managers to incorporate potential future effects of climate on species and habitat into management plans. They allow complex information to be condensed into predictions relevant to natural resource managers. Before this can happen, managers and researchers must determine the structure and goal of the vulnerability assessment (Fig. 1.2). Managers can target an array of organisms or habitats depending on their specific need. For some, the implications of climate change in the immediate future are most relevant to ongoing activities, whereas long-term changes to structure and function of habitats may have relevance to future development and conservation plans. Assessments of vulnerability to climate change necessarily require some knowledge or prediction of response to expected conditions. These predictions, which can be obtained from a wide range of methods, then need to be translated into some measure of the vulnerability that informs management how and why a negative impact is expected to occur. The specific form of these elements depends on the goals of those designing the assessment. In summary, vulnerability assessment involves several steps:

(1) Select a target, scope, and scale.

(2) Predict climate change response.

(3) Translate response into vulnerability.

(4) Glean management implications.

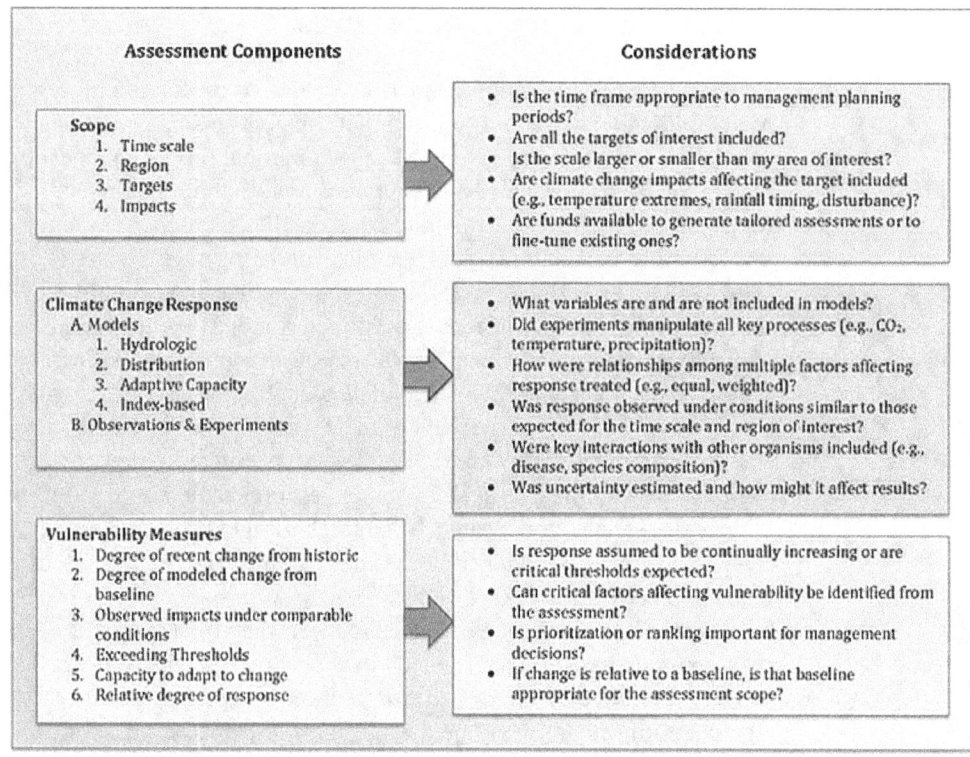

Assessment Components

Scope
1. Time scale
2. Region
3. Targets
4. Impacts

Climate Change Response
A. Models
1. Hydrologic
2. Distribution
3. Adaptive Capacity
4. Index-based
B. Observations & Experiments

Vulnerability Measures
1. Degree of recent change from historic
2. Degree of modeled change from baseline
3. Observed impacts under comparable conditions
4. Exceeding Thresholds
5. Capacity to adapt to change
6. Relative degree of response

Considerations

- Is the time frame appropriate to management planning periods?
- Are all the targets of interest included?
- Is the scale larger or smaller than my area of interest?
- Are climate change impacts affecting the target included (e.g., temperature extremes, rainfall timing, disturbance)?
- Are funds available to generate tailored assessments or to fine-tune existing ones?

- What variables are and are not included in models?
- Did experiments manipulate all key processes (e.g., CO_2, temperature, precipitation)?
- How were relationships among multiple factors affecting response treated (e.g., equal, weighted)?
- Was response observed under conditions similar to those expected for the time scale and region of interest?
- Were key interactions with other organisms included (e.g., disease, species composition)?
- Was uncertainty estimated and how might it affect results?

- Is response assumed to be continually increasing or are critical thresholds expected?
- Can critical factors affecting vulnerability be identified from the assessment?
- Is prioritization or ranking important for management decisions?
- If change is relative to a baseline, is that baseline appropriate for the assessment scope?

Figure 1.2. An overview of assessment components and some key considerations for designing or applying a vulnerability assessment. An assessment will include all elements of scope (reviewed Chapter 2) and one or more measures of response (Chapter 3) and vulnerability (Chapter 4).

These steps, whether or not they are highlighted explicitly, are key components of all vulnerability assessments. The chapters that follow discuss how assessments target appropriate subjects and scope (Chapter 2). In Chapter 3, we cover the tools and methods commonly used to predict climate change response and then discuss how to translate that response into vulnerability (Chapter 4). Finally, we synthesize the use and application of climate change vulnerability assessments conducted for the southwestern United States (Chapter 5).

1.5 Vulnerability Assessments in Natural Resource Management

Many natural resource agencies are conducting vulnerability assessments at various levels of sophistication and for different purposes, often in relation to agency strategic plans and requirements. As an example, the USDA Forest Service has developed a National Roadmap for Responding to Climate Change (USDA Forest Service 2011) based on its strategic framework (USDA Forest Service 2009). The Scorecard identifies vulnerability assessment and adaptation as 2 of 10 elements in four dimensions of accountability for responding to climate change (Box 1.1).

Managers must be able to respond "yes" to 7 of the 10 elements, posed as questions, in the agency's "performance scorecard." The vulnerability assessment question, "Has the Unit engaged in developing relevant information about the vulnerability of key resources, such as human communities and ecosystem elements, to the impacts of climate change?" can be answered through a variety of approaches. Another element focused on adaptation is linked to vulnerability: "Does the Unit conduct management actions that reduce the vulnerability of resources and places to climate change?"

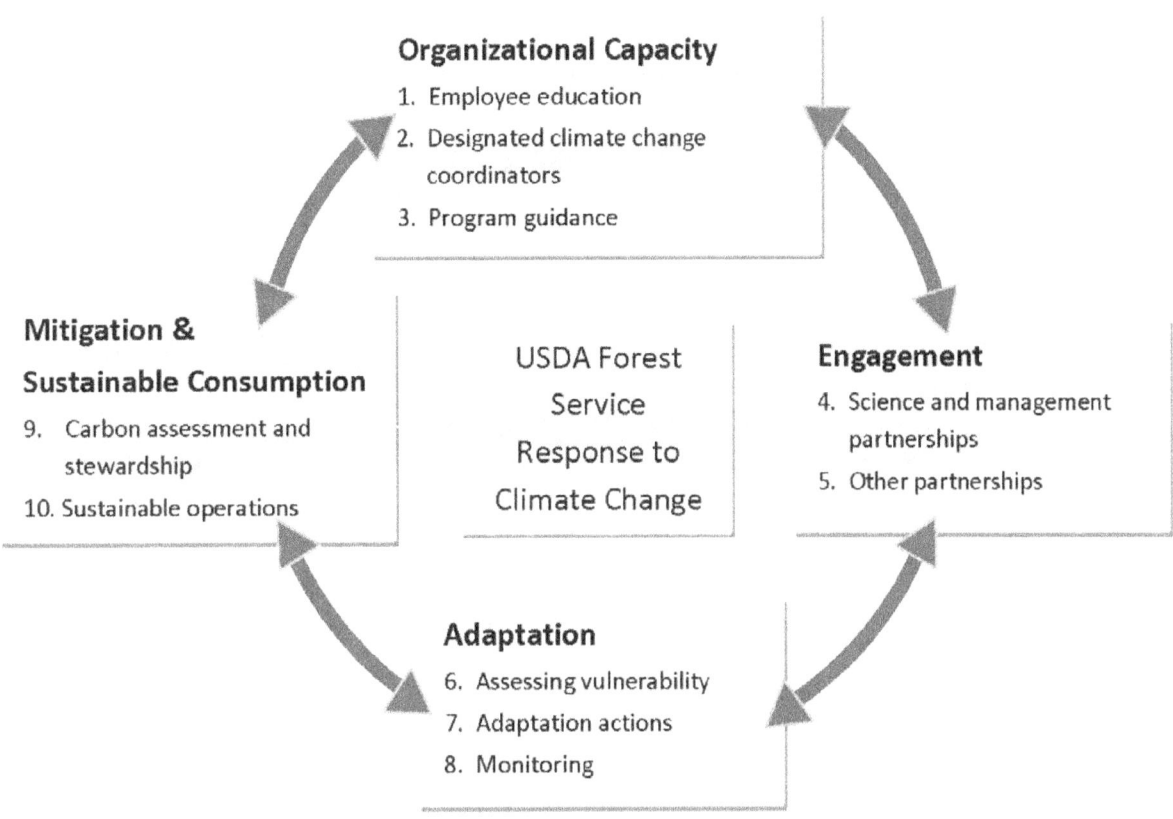

Organizational Capacity

1. Employee education
2. Designated climate change coordinators
3. Program guidance

Engagement

4. Science and management partnerships
5. Other partnerships

USDA Forest Service Response to Climate Change

Mitigation & Sustainable Consumption

9. Carbon assessment and stewardship
10. Sustainable operations

Adaptation

6. Assessing vulnerability
7. Adaptation actions
8. Monitoring

Box 1.1. Forest Service Climate Change Performance Scorecard (USDA Forest Service 2011).

Forest Service units have addressed vulnerability in different ways. Some Forests have assessed vulnerability at the species level using such tools as the NatureServe's Climate Change Index (Young and others 2010), the SAVS questionnaire (e.g., Bagne and others 2011) and more, while other forests have assessed vulnerability at the watershed or landscape level (e.g., Box 1.2). The species and landscape levels have been combined in some assessments (e.g., Box 1.3) to locate geographical areas where multiple species and the area itself are vulnerable. Following the four steps outlined in section 1.4 helps units get to "yes" in assessing vulnerability. These steps as well as our review of considerations, methods, and examples that follow in the next four chapters should be useful for any agency or stakeholder interested in learning about and performing vulnerability assessments.

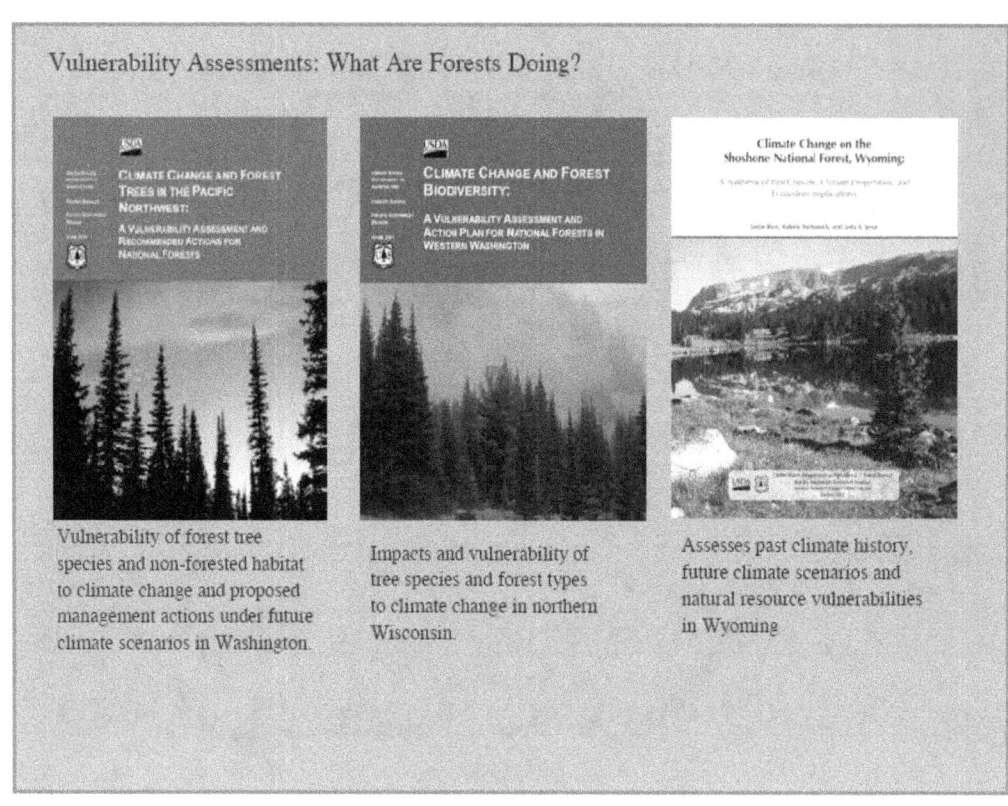

Box 1.2. Examples of vulnerability assessments conducted on forests.

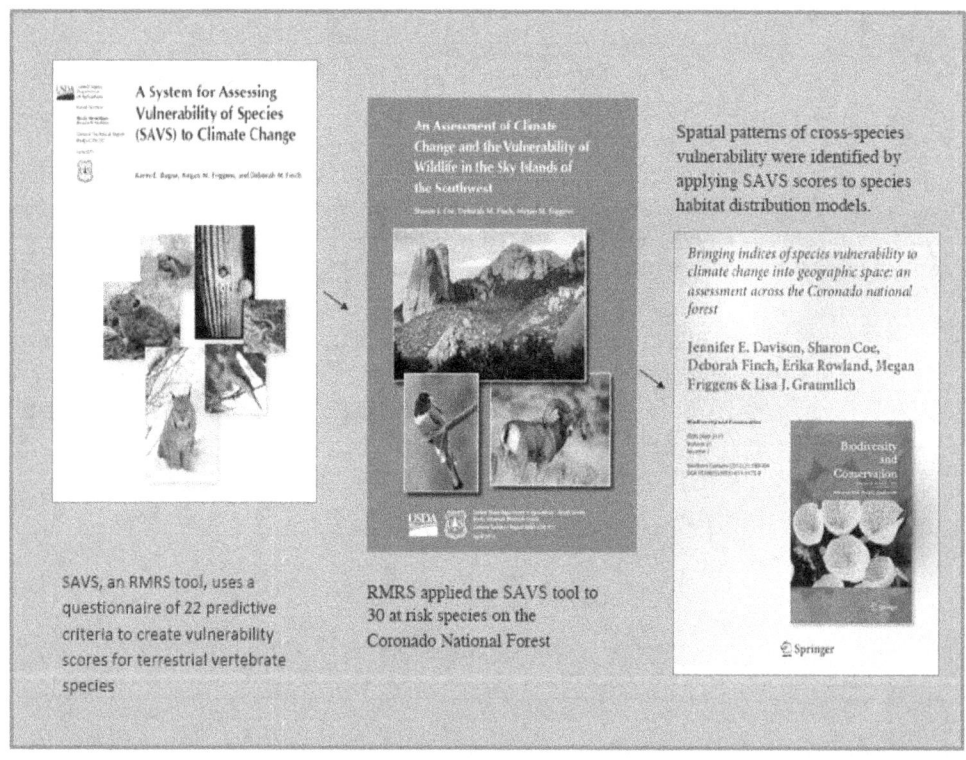

Box 1.3. Reports showing applications of the SAVS tool at the species and landscape levels for the Coronado National Forest.

Literature Cited

Bader, D.C., C. Covey, W.J. Gutowski, Jr., I.M. Held, K.E. Kunkel, R.L. Miller, R.T. Tokmakian, and M.H. Zhang. 2008. Climate Models: An Assessment of Strengths and Limitations. A Report by the U.S. Climate Change Science Program and the Subcommittee on Global Change Research. Department of Energy, Office of Biological and Environmental Research, Washington, DC, USA. 124 pp.

Füssel, H., and R. Klein. 2006. Climate Change Vulnerability Assessments: An Evolution of Conceptual Thinking. Climatic Change 75: 301-329.

Glick, P., B.A. Stein, and N.A. Edelson, eds. 2011. Scanning the conservation horizon: a guide to climate change vulnerability assessment. National Wildlife Federation, Washington, DC.

Harwood, J. 2000. Risk assessment and decision analysis in conservation. Biological Conservation 95: 219-226.

Iverson, Louis R., M.W. Schwartz, and Anantha M. Prasad. 2004. Potential colonization of newly available tree-species habitat under climate change: an analysis for five eastern US species. Landscape Ecology 19: 787-799.

Jenni, L., and M. Kery. 2003. Timing of autumn bird migration under climate change: advances in long–distance migrants, delays in short–distance migrants. Proceedings of the Royal Society, London 270: 1467-1471.

Jones, R. 2001. An Environmental Risk Assessment/Management Framework for Climate Change Impact Assessments. Natural Hazards 23: 197-230.

Parmesan, C. 2006. Ecological and Evolutionary Responses to Recent Climate Change. Annual Review of Ecology, Evolution, and Systematics 37: 637-669.

Peterson, D.L., C.I. Millar, L.A. Joyce, M.J. Furniss, J.E. Halofsky, R.P. Neilson, and T.L. Morelli. 2011. Responding to climate change in National Forests: a guidebook for developing adaptation options. USDA Forest Service, Pacific Northwest Research Station, Gen. Tech. Rep. PNW-GTR-855.

Schmitz, O.J., E. Post, C.E. Burns, and K.M. Johnston. 2003. Ecosystem Responses to Global Climate Change: Moving Beyond Color Mapping. BioScience, 53(12):1199-1205.

Smith, J.B., S.H. Schneider, M. Oppenheimer, [and others]. 2009. Assessing dangerous climate change through an update of the Intergovernmental Panel on Climate Change (IPCC) "reasons for concern." Proceedings of the National Academy of Sciences 106:4133-4137.

Solomon, S., D. Quin, M. Manning, eds. 2007. Climate change 2007: the physical science basis. Contribution of working group I to the fourth assessment report of the Intergovernmental Panel on Climate Change. Cambridge University Press, Cambridge, UK.

U.S. Global Change Research Program [USGCRP]. 2011. Uses of vulnerability assessments for the National Climate Assessment. U.S. National Climate Assessment, Report 9.

USDA Forest Service. 2007. Strategic Plan FY 2007-2012, United States Department of Agriculture, Forest Service, FS-880. Available at: http://www.fs.fed.us/publications/strategic/fs-sp-fy07-12.pdf.

USDA Forest Service. 2011. Navigating the Climate Change Performance Scorecard. A Guide for National Forest and Grasslands, Version 2. Available at: http://www.fs.fed.us/climatechange/advisor/scorecard/scorecard-guidance-08-2011.pdf.

Chapter 2. Targets, Scope, and Scale

Chapter 2 Talking Points

Considerations for evaluating or designing a vulnerability assessment:

(1) What is the target or targets of assessment?
(2) What aspect of the target was or can be measured to estimate vulnerability?
(3) What geographic region does this assessment apply to?
(4) What time scale applies to the predicted changes?
(5) How are interactions across scales addressed?
(6) How do the target, scope, and scale of the assessment affect its application to my management questions?

Managers must consider their objectives and goals in order to design an assessment that will fulfill information needs. Vulnerability assessments are diverse and selection of individual assessments presents a variety of tradeoffs for users (Table 2.1). Assessments are often limited by the type and form of climate change impacts they consider and apply only to limited targeted region areas and time periods. Planning timelines, mandates for resource management, and availability of information all contribute to the initial selection of targets, and the scope, and scale of an individual assessment.

2.1 Assessment Targets

Climate change has the potential to affect the entire range of human and natural systems, so a key aspect of a vulnerability assessment is selecting what population, species, functional group, process, or ecosystem will be addressed. Quantifiable

Table 2.1. Relevance of spatial scale for assessing vulnerability to climate change (from Peterson and others 2011).

	Spatial scale		
	Large[a]	Intermediate[b]	Small[c]
Availability of information on climate and climate change effects	High for future climate and general effects on vegetation and water	Moderate for river systems, vegetation, and animals	High for resource data, low for climate change
Accuracy of predictions of climate change effects	High	Moderate to high	High for temperature and water, low to moderate for other resources
Usefulness for specific projects	Generally not relevant	Relevant for forest density management, fuel treatment, wildlife, and fisheries	Can be useful if confident that information can be downscaled accurately
Usefulness for planning	High if collaboration across management units is effective	High for a wide range of applications	Low to moderate

[a] More than 10,000 km^2 (e.g., basin, multiple National Forests)
[b] 100 to 10,000 km^2 (e.g., subbasin, National Forest, Ranger District)
[c] Less than 100 km^2 (e.g., watershed)

aspects of the target as they relate to management objectives will determine the variable upon which vulnerability measures are based. For example, population growth rates could be used to assess a group of frog species at risk of extinction and stream flow would be an appropriate variable for a target watershed that provides water to urban or agricultural areas. Vulnerability assessments are most useful when they address the critical needs of managers or conservationists. A wide range of assessment targets, from individuals or populations to landscapes and processes, can be evaluated for vulnerability. Targets represent the resource value of interest and will depend on management objectives, but targets will also be constrained by policies, budgets, and available information (see Chapter 4, Table 4.1). Important considerations for target selection include the available information regarding potential system or species to be assessed, the time line of desired outcomes, and the specific objectives of the user. The audience for which the vulnerability assessment is being prepared and the input of stakeholders can also be important considerations for selecting targets (Glick and others 2011). If the target is a single subject (e.g., one species, one watershed), the purpose of a vulnerability assessment is to dissect the nature of expected impacts to that target. When the target includes multiple subjects (e.g., plant functional groups, watersheds of Oregon, and endangered species), ranking or prioritization of the subjects is possible along with information on the particular vulnerabilities of the individual subjects. There are also new efforts to integrate vulnerability across multiple targets or sectors to get a more complete picture of vulnerability (USGCRP 2011). When using assessment results to generate management strategies, it is critical to consider how and why targets were selected to ensure that the information provided by the assessment is used appropriately.

Limitations in data availability influence the feasibility of assessing of particular targets. Data limitations reduce the applicability of many types of vulnerability assessments. For example, although species' vulnerability can be assessed with minimal data in some situations (Bagne and others 2011), a relatively complete understanding of species biology provides better prediction of response and thus a better approximation of vulnerability. Response of broader plant functional groups or community types (e.g., mixed-conifer forest, semi-arid shrubland, and grasslands) can be very useful for managers because they encompass many whole-system properties that may be missed when single species are the focus of assessment. Similarly, estimates of climate change effects for ecosystem processes, which are very useful for identifying fundamental large-scale vulnerability, require a great deal of data and an understanding of complex dynamics among multiple contributing components. Though vulnerability assessments will be most useful and applicable when used on systems that have adequate data, assessments that focus on more general targets are possible and still valuable where data are limited.

2.2 Scope

Assessments are generally prepared for a specific geographic region and time period. The scope of the assessment considers both temporal and spatial scale, which will be determined by the availability of suitable input data, the management unit, selected assessment target(s), and timeline for management planning. For natural resource managers, management units and jurisdiction often dictate the focal region. Time scale is an important aspect of climate projections that affects application to management goals. Management strategies may focus on short-term goals relating to preserving or restoring current conditions or on long-term goals that aim to maintain ecosystem function and stability over time. These distinct temporal components naturally lead to different targets and objectives for a vulnerability assessment. Scope also applies to the range of stressors used (i.e., the source of vulnerability) in the assessment because climate change includes not just temperature and precipitation but also related phenomena such as stream flow, erosion, disturbance (fire and insect outbreaks), and extreme weather events. Therefore, the range of climate-related stressors considered can be quite broad and encompass multiple interrelated stressors or focus more narrowly on a single stressor of interest (e.g., drought, sea level rise) that has a strong effect on the target. Inclusion of non-climate change stressors can also broaden scope of the assessment.

Difficulties arise when the temporal and spatial scales of available data are limited and/or differ from the desired scope of the assessment. Available data such as outputs from climate models are scale limited and generally much larger than typical management units. To produce projections at finer scales, many downscaling methods are available for climate projections. The most commonly used approaches are dynamic (in which climate physics and chemistry are modeled at regional scales, in the same way used in General Circulation Models or GCMs), and statistical downscaling, which is accomplished by interpolating coarser resolution GCM data using a variety of spatial statistical methods. Downscaling brings climate projections to a spatial scale that can be very useful for managers (e.g., 25 km^2 grid cells). Downscaling can also correct regional bias found in many global climate projections and is inherent to results of efforts to produce projections that are averaged across multiple climate models (Bader and others 2008). However, these methods, along with the unknown progression of greenhouse gas inputs, add error, which contributes to variability and uncertainty in the predictions made by a vulnerability assessment.

Figure 2.1. Adapted from Poiani and others 2000. Biodiversity at various spatial scales. Levels of biological organization include ecosystems and species. Ecosystems and species are defined at four geographic scales: local, intermediate, coarse, and regional. The general range in hectares for each spatial scale is indicated (left of pyramid), as are common characteristics of ecosystems and species at each of the spatial scales (right of pyramid).

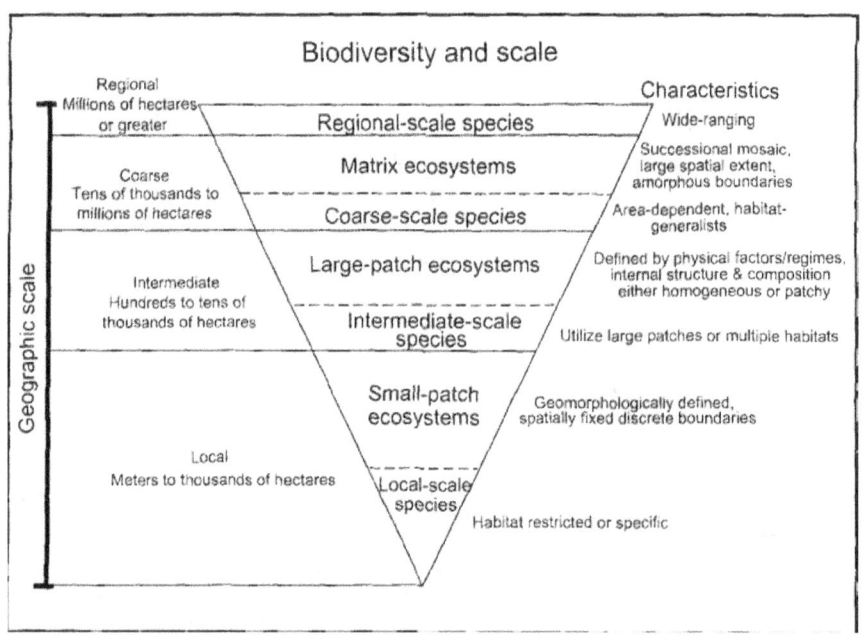

2.3 Biological Scale

Biological scales range from the levels of genomes and species (e.g., Durance and Ormerod 2007; Triepke and others 2012) to continent-scale ecological biomes (e.g., Rehfeldt and others 2012) (Fig. 2.1). The appropriate scale depends on the target defined for the vulnerability assessment, as mentioned in the previous section. Furthermore, assessments may include evaluation targets across multiple scales or cross-scale. Both spatial and temporal scales may be considered simultaneously with any given biological entity. Time scales vary from years (e.g., Allen and Breshears 1995) to a century or more (e.g., Parmesan and Yohe 2003), while spatial scales vary from individual niches and biotic communities (e.g., Hofstetter and others 2007) to intercontinental levels (Allen 2009). From the standpoint of conservation biology, biological scales are typically expressed simultaneously in terms of space and time. It is important to understand how biological processes operate across a range of spatial and temporal scales and how those processes are ultimately manifested in biological diversity.

Biological scales provide key concepts in linking temporal and spatial—local, regional, and biogeographical—scales where dynamics are driven by climate change. For example, the effects of landscape homogenization, as a result of warmer temperatures and uncharacteristic fires, are sometimes treated as static when, in reality, the spatial effects of changing landscape patterns on the distribution of specific species may be apparent only at the population level. Spatial responses of populations and metapopulations to disturbances must be understood and quantified at a range of spatial scales concurrently with the frequencies and intensities of disturbance.

Here, we provide a brief look at biological scale in respect to conservation issues and climate change. Biological scales are an initial response to management or research inquiries—for example, "how will climate change projections affect the willow flycatcher?" At broader scales, one might ask "where is pinyon die-off most likely?" At continental scales, "what is the potential range of suitable habitat for Douglas-fir 100 years from now?" While there is a considerable range of biological scales, we briefly consider two—species and ecosystems. We then present a review of the Forest Service landscape analysis, which provides an example of one way in which an assessment manages scope and scale.

2.3.1 Species Scale

Individual species are a common concern for managers and researchers in regard to climate change vulnerability, and their response will filter up to targets at broader scales. Species often reflect a familiar operational level and a suitable biological scale, given that species protection is fundamental to conservation and is embedded in core mandates of Federal agencies (e.g., 7 USC § 136, 16 U.S.C. § 1531 et seq.). The rationale for these mandates is that those species that are sensitive to climate change can be identified, their locations and habitats can be catalogued and mapped, and species can be managed through protective habitat measures, including adaptation (Millar and others 2007). The Nature Conservancy identified approximately 120 plant and animal species in the Southwest that are at risk according to the habitats most vulnerable to climate change (Robles and Enquist 2011). Problems arise at the species scale because of sparse information on the vast majority of species.

2.3.2 Ecosystem Scale

Ecosystems are the relevant biological scale for application of coarse filter methodology, which estimates biodiversity based largely on environmental factors (Cushman and others 2008). Like species, ecosystem entities are familiar to managers and researchers alike, in regard to ecological analysis and conservation strategies. While definitions for ecosystem vary, in general, ecosystems consist of biota that share common habitat features, biogeography, and climate, making them a particularly relevant biological scale for the evaluation of climate change.

Ecosystems, however, are problematic to delineate. Ecosystems are far from homogenous, spatially or temporally, and are a dynamic and shifting mixture of various stages of ecological succession whose expression in time and space bear on biological development and disturbance patterns. Nevertheless, ecosystems are often mapped to facilitate vulnerability assessment and ecological analysis (Cleland and others 2007; Triepke and others 2008). Once mapped, key questions are posed for those evaluating the effects of climate change at the ecosystem scale: (1) to what extent are ecosystems affected by climate change in regards to their natural functioning; and (2) how can ecosystem function be accommodated through adaptation strategies for the persistence of the species that ecosystems contain (via coarse filter analysis). Landscape analysis, for which the ecosystem scale is most associated with, is discussed in the next section.

2.4 Case Study: Landscape Analysis

Following is a summary of landscape analysis in the context of climate change and vulnerability assessment. This is not an exhaustive overview, but rather a description of common features found in landscape analyses, particular those of the USDA Forest Service (e.g., USDA Forest Service 2006). The biological scale most easily adapted to landscape-scale analysis is the ecosystem level discussed in the previous section; however, a landscape analysis provides the requisite coarse-filter framework for the analysis of fine-filter elements (Cushman and others 2008), including individual species of concern and interest. Unlike biological scale, the scales associated with landscape analyses are usually spatially and temporally explicit. Within the Forest Service, landscape analysis normally includes three interdependent sustainability components, ecological, social, and economic, though the focus here is on the ecological component.

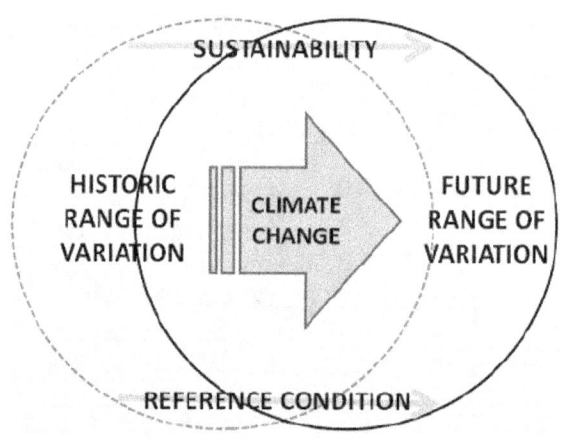

Box 2.1. Direction of change from historic to future range of variation

Another factor common to landscape analyses of the Forest Service is the application of a reference condition–a benchmark range of conditions that reflect ecological sustainability for a given attribute (FRCC 2010). Reference condition concepts, including their importance in evaluating sustainability, have not been lost on the Forest Service's new Planning Rule (2012), though the definition of reference condition is shifting in light of climate change (see Box 2.1). The Forest Service recognizes that as ecosystem potentials shift with changing climate that the historic range of variation, often used to help describe the reference condition, may lose significance. Either way, in the course of landscape analysis, reference conditions are typically identified for key attributes of vegetation community structure and composition, disturbance regimes, and other attributes that collectively reflect ecosystem structure, function, and process.

In sum, landscape analysis usually involves: (1) the selection of appropriate attributes along with spatial and temporal scales for analysis; (2) describing the reference condition, current condition, and trends of ecosystem attributes; and (3) analyzing the status of those attributes, often as departure from reference conditions (USDA Forest Service 2006).

2.4.1 Ecosystem Attributes

Ecosystem attributes should be meaningful for the characterization of structure, function, and process, and meaningful to past, current, or future management. Ecosystem abundance and diversity, for instance, are often described by quantifying successional states, each state delineated by their differences in structure and composition—canopy cover class, size class, dominance type (Triepke and others 2005). The proportion of successional stages is compared among reference, current, and future conditions. Both reference and future conditions are often identified through landscape simulation models (Weisz and others 2009, 2010), using different parameterizations for the type, frequency, and severity of disturbance. The degree to which current and reference conditions differ, or to which future and reference conditions differ, is shown in tabular summaries and expressed in departure index values where lower departure reflects a greater degree of ecological sustainability.

Other ecosystem attributes involve major disturbances. For instance, the frequency of fire, both wildfire and planned ignitions, is quantified by each severity class (non-lethal, mixed severity, and stand replacement). Here again, comparisons are made between current and reference conditions, or future and reference conditions. Insect and disease agents are likewise quantified by frequency and severity for forest and woodland systems (e.g., Lynch and others 2008). Other major disturbance processes include herbivory, erosion, and flooding.

Spatial attributes are not often evaluated with landscape analyses, though we recognize the importance of evaluating landscape metrics such as patch size, connectivity, interior forest, and other spatial features significant to the biota of an area (Forman and Godron 1986). Though various geographic information systems (GIS) and spatial analysis tool exist for quantitative analysis (McGarigal and Marks 1995), the difficulty has often been in establishing reference conditions for each ecosystem from which to assess sustainability. Sometimes uncharacteristic levels of fragmentation are simply assumed so that analysis is relegated to a comparison of management scenarios and their ability to affect landscape connectivity.

To fully address climate change, much more sophisticated landscape simulation models are necessary, models that can project vegetation patterns based on future climate and along with growth and disturbance patterns in natural plant communities (Bachelet and others 2001). These models have has limited application in the Southwest but will be needed not only to project ecosystem conditions but to reestablish reference conditions. Reference conditions of the future will reflect shifting site potential patterns, biological migrations, and new disturbance potentials.

2.4.2 Cross-Scale Applications

Any one of the attributes mentioned above can be analyzed at multiple scales. As an example, Forest Plan revision analyses that were conducted in the Southwestern Region (USDA Forest Service 2006) focused on three nesting scales—ecological sections (Cleland and others 2007), Plan Unit (e.g., at the scale of a National Forest or National Grassland), and ecological subsections. These three scales have been used successfully to assess overall ecological sustainability at the scale of the Plan Unit, to identify diversity patterns within the Plan Unit (i.e., a comparison among subsections), and to assess the Plan Unit in reference to contiguous ecological sections. The analysis of ecological sections provides planners and managers a means to determine conservation burden, for instance where ecosystem conditions are degraded within other ownerships of the same section for a given ecosystem type. Multi-scalar analysis is likewise important for cross-scale interactions that can occur with climate change. The diversity within some plant communities, for example, may actually increase by the effects of climate change and subsequent invasion by novel plant and animal components, while the overall diversity of an area may be in decline at upward spatial scales.

While a particular biologic scale may be suited to the chosen target, it is important to simultaneously consider other scales when interpreting a vulnerability assessment (Table 2.1). Linking biological scales is necessary if a conservation concern occurs at a scale different from its solution. For example, climate change is occurring at scales of entire biomes, but the required adaptation strategies for fragmented landscapes are more likely to be applied at the scales of individual ecosystems and ecoregions (Cleland and others 2007). Research and analysis resulting from the application of different biological scales has shown different patterns of vulnerability. For instance, increases in diversity may occasionally occur at the population scale as driven by climate change (Bale and others 2002) but may contradict patterns at ecosystem or biome scales where diversity is in decline. While many vulnerability assessments consider the scale effect, its inclusion in practice is largely missing from the range of studies regarding ecological effect of climate change and results from multiple scales are seldom explicitly addressed. Others argue that landscape scales are requisite for fully determining cross-scale patterns (e.g., Stevens and others 2006), admittedly making assessment more complicated. Interactive effects and disturbance regimes are covered in greater detail in Chapter 3.

Literature Cited

Allen, C.D. 2009. Climate-induced forest dieback: An escalating global phenomenon? Unasylva 231/232 60(1-2): 43-49.

Allen, C.D., and D.D. Breshears. 1995. A drought-induced shift in a forest/woodland ecotone: rapid response to variation in climate. Supplement to Bulletin of the Ecological Society of America 76(2): 3.

Allen, C.D., and D.D. Breshears. 1998. Drought-induced shift of a forest-woodland ecotone: Rapid response to climate variation. Proceedings of the National Academy of Sciences U.S. 95(25): 14839-14842.

Andersen, T., J. Carstensen, E. Hernandez-Garcia, and C.M. Duarte. 2008. Ecological thresholds and regime shifts: approaches to identification. Trends in Ecology and Evolution 24(1): 49-57.

Bachelet, D., J.M. Lenihan, C. Daly, R.P. Neilson, D.S. Ojima, and W.J. Parton. 2001. MC1—A dynamic vegetation model for estimating the distribution of vegetation and associated ecosystem fluxes of carbon, nutrient, and water. Gen. Tech. Rep. PNW-GTR-508. Corvallis, OR: USDA Forest Service, Forest Service, Pacific Northwest Research Station.

Bagne, K.E., M.M. Friggens, and D.M. Finch. 2011. A system for assessing vulnerability of species (SAVS) to climate change. Gen. Tech. Rep. RMRS-GTR-257. Fort Collins, CO: USDA Forest Service, Rocky Mountain Research Station.

Bale, J.S., G.J. Masters, I.D. Hodkinson, [and others]. 2002. Herbivory in global climate change research: direct effects of rising temperature on insect herbivores. Global Change Biology 8: 1-16.

Breshears, D.D., [and others]. 2005. Regional vegetation die-off in response to global-change-type drought. Proceedings of the National Academy of Sciences U.S. 102(42): 15144-15148.

Cleland, D.T., J.A. Freeouf, G.J. Nowacki, C. Carpenter, J.E. Keys, and W.H. McNab. 2007. Ecological subregions: Sections and subsections of the conterminous United States. USDA Forest Service, Washington Office, Washington, DC. 1:3,500,000 scale geodatabase available at: http://fsweb.wo.fs.fed.us/em/rig/index.html.

Cushman, S.A., K.S. McKelvey, C.H. Flather, and K. McGarigal. 2008. Do forest community types provide a sufficient basis to evaluate biological diversity? Frontiers in Ecology and the Environment 6: 13-17.

Durance, I., and S.J. Ormerod. 2007. Climate change effects on upland stream macroinvertebrates over a 25-year period. Global Change Biology 13: 942-957.

Fire Regime Condition Class [FRCC]. 2010. Interagency fire regime condition class guidebook, v. 3.0. National Interagency Fuels, Fire, & Vegetation Technology Transfer guide. Available at: www.frcc.gov.

Flannigan, M., B. Stocks, and B. Wotton. 2000. Climate change and forest fires. The Science of the Total Environment 262:221-229.

Forman, R.T.T., and M. Godron. 1986. Landscape ecology. New York: John Wiley & Sons.

Hobbs, R. J., Higgs, E., and Harris, J. A. 2009. Novel ecosystems: implications for conservation and restoration. Trends in Ecology and Evolution 24: 599-605.

Hofstetter, R.W., T.D. Dempsey, K.D. Klepzig, and M.P. Ayres. Temperature-dependent effects on mutualistic, antagonistic, and commensalistic interactions among insects, fungi, and mites. Community Ecology 8: 47-56.

Kitzberger T., E. Araoz, J.H. Gowda, M. Mermoz, and J.M. Morales. 2011. Decreases in fire spread probability with forest age promote alternative community states, reduced resilience to climate variability and large fire regime shifts. Ecosystems DOI: 10.1007/s10021-011-9494-y.

Lentile, L., P. Morgan, A. Hudak, M. Bobbitt, S. Lewis, A. Smith, and P. Robichaud. 2007. Post-fire burn severity and vegetation response following eight large wildfires across the western United States. Fire Ecology 3: 91-108.

Loehman, R.A., J.A. Clark, and R.E. Keane. 2011. Modeling Effects of Climate Change and Fire Management on Western White Pine (*Pinus monticola*) in the Northern Rocky Mountains, USA. Forests 2: 832-860.

Lynch, A.M., J.A Anhold, J.D. McMillin, S.M. Dudley, R.A. Fitzgibbon, and M.L. Fairweather. 2008. Forest insect & disease activity on the Prescott NF 1918-2006. USDA Forest Service unpublished technical report on file. Rocky Mountain Research Station and Southwestern Region. Tucson, AZ.

Mayer, A.L., and A.H. Khalanyi. 2011. Grass trumps trees with fire. Science 334: 188-189.

McGarigal, K., and B.J. Marks. 1995. FRAGSTATS: Spatial analysis program for quantifying landscape structure. Oregon State University technical guide. Corvallis, OR.

Millar, C.I., N.I. Stephenson, and S.L. Stephens. 2007. Climate change and forests of the future: Managing in the face of uncertainty. Ecological Applications 17: 2145-2151.

Opdam, P., and D. Wascher. 2004. Climate change meets habitat fragmentation: linking landscape and biogeographical scale levels in research and conservation. Biological Conservation 117: 285-297.

Overpeck J.T., D. Rind, and R. Goldberg. 1990. Climate-induced changes in forest disturbance and vegetation. Nature 343: 51-53.

Parmesan, C., and G. Yohe. A globally coherent fingerprint of climate change impacts across natural systems. Nature 421: 37-42.

Rehfeldt, G.E., N.L. Crookston, C. Saenz-Romero, and E.M. Campbell. 2012. North American vegetation model for land-use planning in a changing climate: a solution to large classification problems. Ecological Applications 22: 119-141.

Rehfeldt, G.E., N.L. Crookston, M.V. Warwell, and J.S. Evans. 2006. Empirical Analyses of Plant-Climate Relationships for the Western United States. International Journal of Plant Sciences 167(6): 1123-1150.

Robles, M., and C. Enquist. 2011. Managing changing landscapes in the southwestern United States. The Nature Conservancy, technical guide. Tucson, AZ.

Savage, M., and J.N. Mast. 2005. How resilient are ponderosa pine ecosystems after crown fires? Canadian Journal of Forest Research 35: 967-977.

Scheffer, M., [and others]. 2001. Catastrophic shifts in ecosystems. Nature 413: 591-596.

Stevens, V.M., C. Verkenne, S. vandewoestijne, R.A. Wesselingh, and M. Baguette. 2006. Gene flow and functional connectivity in the natterjack toad. Molecular Ecology 15: 2333-2344.

Symrnioudis, I., A.D. Watt, and J.B. Whittaker. 2002. Herbivory in global climate change research: direct effects of rising temperatures on insect herbivores. Global Change Biology 8: 1-16.

Triepke, F.J., C.K. Brewer, D.M. Leavell, and S.J. Novak. 2008. Mapping forest alliances and associations using fuzzy systems and nearest neighbor classifiers. Remote Sensing of Environment 112(3): 1037-1050.

Triepke, F.J., T.E. DeMeo, M. Al Otoum, and L. Al-Azzam. 2012. Composition and structure of Aleppo pine (*Pinus halepensis*) communities in the Dibeen Forest Reserve, Jordan. Natural Areas Journal 32(4): 356-366.

Triepke, F.J., W.A. Robbie, and T.C. Mellin. 2005. Dominance type classification—Existing vegetation classification for the Southwestern Region. Forestry Report FR-R3-16-1. Albuquerque, NM: USDA Forest Service.

U.S. Global Change Research Program [USGCRP]. 2011. Uses of vulnerability assessments for the National Climate Assessment. U.S. National Climate Assessment, Report 9.

USDA Forest Service. 2006. Ecological sustainability: Developing a framework for ecological sustainability on National Forest Lands and National Grasslands in the Southwestern Region, v. 4.11. Unpublished USDA Forest Service technical guide on file. Southwestern Region, Regional Office, Albuquerque, NM.

Weisz, R., F.J. Triepke, and R. Truman. 2009. Evaluating the ecological sustainability a ponderosa pine ecosystem on the Kaibab Plateau in Northern Arizona. Fire Ecology 5:114-128.

Weisz, R., F.J. Triepke, D. Vandendriesche, M. Manthei, J. Youtz, J. Simon, and W. Robbie. 2010. Evaluating the ecological sustainability of a piñon-juniper grassland ecosystem in northern Arizona. Pp. 321-336 in: T. B. Jain, R. T. Graham, and J. Sandquist, eds., Proceedings of the 2009 National Silviculture Workshop, 15-19 June 2009, Boise, ID. Proc. RMRS-P-61. Fort Collins, CO: USDA Forest Service, Rocky Mountain Research Station.

Westerling, A.L., H.G. Hidalgo, D.R. Cayan, and T.W. Swetnam. 2006. Warming and earlier spring increase western U.S. wildfire activity. Science 313 (5789): 940-943.

Zinck, R.D., M. Pascual, and V. Grimm. 2011. Understanding shifts in wildfire regimes as emergent threshold phenomena. American Naturalist 178(6): E149-E161.

Chapter 3. Predicting Response to Climate Change

Chapter 3 Talking Points

(1) **All approaches are limited by the input data available.**
(2) **Like assessments, analysis of response is generally limited to a particular target, scope, and scale.**
(3) **Be aware of assumptions and limitations in predictive methodologies.**
(4) **Anticipate tipping points, interactive effects, and uncertainty even if not addressed by assessments.**
(5) **The future is always uncertain but methods vary in their capacity to address it.**

3.1 Introduction

A variety of methods have been developed to explore how climate change will affect basic biological processes, ecological function, population dynamics, and/ or species composition. Although the focus of a vulnerability assessment is often negative or undesirable impacts to valued resources, response can cover the full range of impacts from negative to positive, and findings of positive effects or resilience can be equally important for informing management decisions (e.g., Bradley 2009, 2010). In this chapter, we review several of the approaches used to measure one or more aspects of response to climate change (Tables 3.1-3.3). We also briefly discuss how frameworks are used in the vulnerability assessment process (Table 3.4).

Climate change predictions are derived from one or more GCMs based on atmospheric physics and ocean-atmosphere interactions, under a multiple predefined greenhouse gas (GHG) scenarios, which estimate future greenhouse gas emissions (Nakićenović and others 2000). The models provide estimates of a wide range of climate variables. This approach naturally lends itself to studies that relate climate response directly to changes in precipitation, temperature, and other variables that are predicted across broad scales of space and time. Indeed, the great majority of analyses that address ecological effects of climate change focus on change in species, community type, or habitat distributions in response to changes in environmental variables. A smaller but important subset of modeling techniques uses aspects of bioenergetic and metapopulation theories to identify relationships between critical processes and climate variables as a measure of impact or vulnerability. Studies using these methods may focus on one element, combine bioenergetics and population analyses, or use them in conjunction with distribution analyses to generate spatially explicit predictions. A second, growing class of studies uses ranking or scoring processes to quantify relative vulnerabilities between groups of species, habitats, or even regions. Climate change impacts to hydrological systems and function are assessed through a variety of methods ranging from watershed models that simulate expected hydrological conditions to more comprehensive methods that include both biotic and abiotic components. Though both terrestrial and aquatic assessments may incorporate similar modeling methods for biological diversity, aquatic assessment methods typically contain an additional emphasis on the physics of natural systems and specific hydrological components.

In the next chapter, we cover how these estimates or measures of response are translated into expected vulnerability and, ultimately, management application.

3.2 General Methods

The following discussion centers on the major approaches used in climate change analyses that inform vulnerability assessments (Tables 3.1, 3.2). As discussed here and in Chapter 1, assessments may use one or more of these approaches or summarize multiple studies to determine relative vulnerability of assessment targets (see Chapter 4). These approaches cover a diverse range of biological and geographic scales (Fig. 3.1) and have unique qualities for addressing management questions. In this chapter, we highlight studies that demonstrate the application of the methods described for estimating response to climate change. However, in most instances, these studies do not represent vulnerability assessments in and of themselves.

Hydrological models include approaches that predict changes in streamflow, water temperature, and quality or other features, such as flood regime and water source, that influence watershed resilience. Hydrological models encompass a variety of mostly statistical approaches that estimate the impact of climate change on water systems and can incorporate both ecological and economical aspects of system vulnerability. Hydrological models often inform other modeling approaches focused on species or biomes. A second group comprises a variety of approaches that model characteristics believed to influence the capacity of species or ecosystems to survive or absorb changes to climate; these are grouped together here under the heading of adaptive capacity models. Adaptive capacity measures are also commonly used in assessments of socio-economic vulnerability and, although relevant to natural resource management, are beyond the scope of this review. The largest group includes distribution models, which encompass a range of approaches to estimate future impact to species/communities/biome distributions (Appendix 1). These models may generate predictions of future habitat suitability for species or communities, future habitat characteristics, patterns of biodiversity, or physiological stress for a single species. Finally, a variety of methods aim to identify the relative vulnerability or priority of targets through a comparison of traits or issues among a group of study subjects. Within this group of tools and methods, we focus on those referred to as index-based measures, which have only recently emerged within the literature and arose in response to limitations in directly measuring vulnerability (Table 3.3). We briefly discuss some of the strengths and weaknesses of each of these approaches (Table 3.2).

3.2.1 Hydrological Models

Hydrological models are a distinct group of models that represent mostly physical processes within an ecosystem. However, this can also refer to models that incorporate other methods (bioenergetic models for instance) to present a comprehensive but water-based estimate of future impact. Hydrological models are considered a distinct group here due to their specialized nature and their application to the field of water related vulnerability assessments (Table 3.2; see Chapter 5). Hydrological models are useful for exploring climate effects on a variety of aquatic and non-aquatic riparian areas. Most models rely on the understanding that many fundamental ecological processes are determined by or related to flow variation (Meyers and others 1999; Guertin and others 2000). Meyers and others (1999)

Table 3.1. A general overview of models and methods used to evaluate vulnerability for climate change assessment.

	Description	Target	Scope and Scale	Examples
1. Hydrological Models	Model changes in ground water, stream flow, evaporation, and productivity and nutrient cycles under various climate scenarios. Can infer trends for both abiotic and biotic systems associated with water.	Water flow, nutrient cycles, productivity	Individual streams to watersheds	Christensen and others 2008
2. Adaptive Capacity Models	Models focus on traits important to species or system persistence under changing conditions, in particular climate change. This may include studies of landscape connectivity, species dispersal, intraspecific genetic variation, or colonizing ability. Alternatively, methods might quantify observed changes to species ranges, reproductive success, or, for larger scales, ecosystem resilience.	Animal or plant adaptive capacity	Species, has been applied to ecosystems	Peery and others 2012
3. Distribution Models				
A. Simulation/Process-based Models	Simulate processes to predict behavior of model target			
Biogeographic Models	Models simulate limiting conditions relating to potential vegetation type using differing climate and hydrological conditions and include measures of transpiration rates, photosynthetic pathway, soils, disturbance, and CO_2.	Plant distributions/primary productivity	Vegetation type	Neilson 1995; IPCC 1996
Biogeochemical Models (BGC)	These models simulate ecosystem process such as photosynthesis, transpiration, litter fall, soil moisture, NPP and nutrient cycling given a set of variables, including temperature, precipitation, solar radiation, soil texture, and CO_2.	NPP, carbon storage	Vegetation type	IPCC report
Dynamic Global Vegetation Models	Combines biogeographic, biogeochemical models, and hydrology and/or disturbance variables to generate estimates on a wide variety of functions. These estimates are then used to create distribution maps of plants (e.g., plant life form).	Plant species composition across study area	Vegetation type, multiple spatial and temporal scales (see text)	McMahon 2011; Notaro and others 2012
GAP Models	Also known as succession or patch models, these add disturbance and explicitly incorporate demographic components (tree growth, competition, and death) to predict probability of species presence.	Plants, Composition, age class, relative abundance	Species composition. Multiple spatial scales; is a temporally dynamic model	

	Description	Target	Scope and Scale	Examples
B. Dynamic Bioenergetic Models	Refers to models that incorporate information on energy budgets to either predict species distribution using assumptions regarding potential energy intake or to estimate individual or population persistence (i.e., extinction probability) under varying conditions when combined with population or metapopulation analysis.	Animal distribution	Animal species/populations	Buckley 2008
C. Niche Theory Models Bioclimate Envelope Models (BCE)	Estimates future distribution based upon current and historical relationships between species/community/life-form occurrence and climate variables. Can be conducted by classification, regression, and other methods (see Box 3.1).	Distribution of Animal, plant, habitat, and biodiversity	Species through ecosystems	Notaro and others 2012
Statistical Species Distribution Models (SSDM)	Predict potential distribution of species and colonization based on statistical relationships rather than empirical data. Uses historical and current climate/site characteristics to inform model. Example: Species distribution as a function of land cover type, scaled biodiversity patterns, species area relationships, etc.	Animal or plant species distribution	Species	Thomas and others 2004
4. Prioritization Methods *A. Conceptual Models*	Qualitative descriptions and diagrams of attributes and processes of concern. Priorities determined through perceived sensitivities, exposure risk, and desired outcome.	Ecosystem and economic resources	Flexible	Heemskerk and others 2003
B. Quantification Tools	Also known as index or scoring tools. Typically quantify vulnerability through a tally of traits or characteristics associated with increased risk of negative impact. Identifies priorities and specific vulnerabilities in study system.	Relative vulnerability of species	Varies	Bagne and others 2011; Young and others 2011
C. Risk Assessments	Often used to consider both socioeconomic and ecological vulnerabilities to climate change. Vary in form from statistical approaches to frameworks.	Relative vulnerability of entity of interest	Flexible	Jones 2001

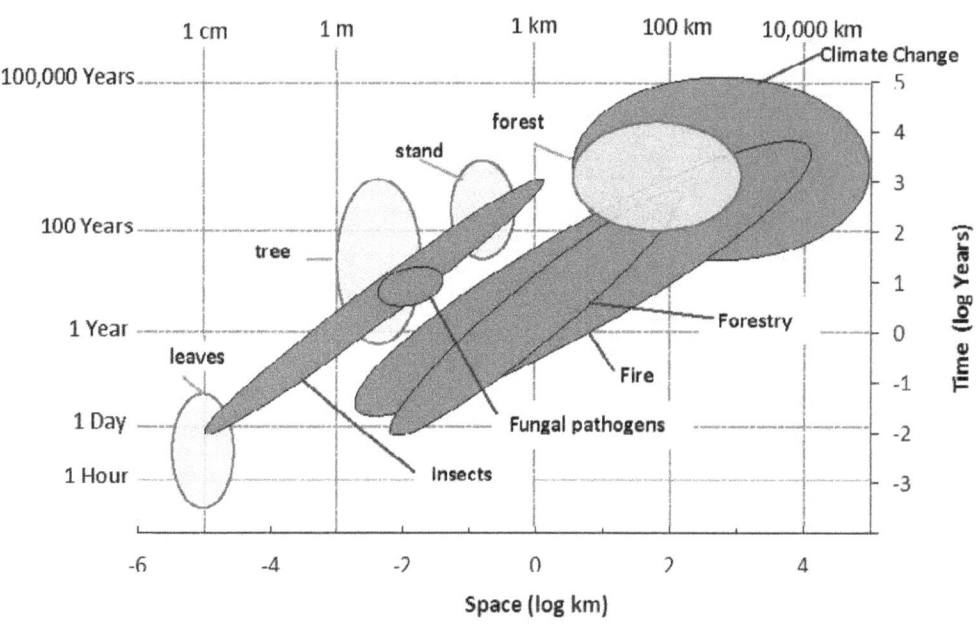

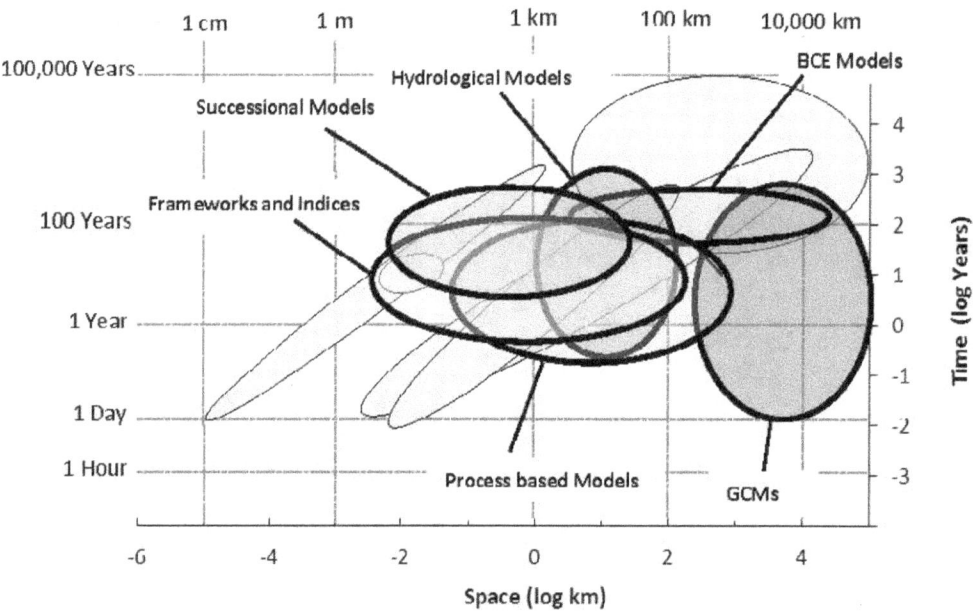

Figure 3.1. Top. Temporal and spatial variation among biological scales (light blue) and the impact of common disturbances (dark blue) for forested ecosystems (patterned after Bunnel and Huggard 1999). See Chapter 2 for a detailed discussion. **Bottom.** Spatial and temporal extent of target ouput for methods for assessing impact of climate change on various ecological parameters. Disturbance parameters (grey) are shown for reference. This figure represents the common geographic scale at which certain analyses are conducted. GCMs (dark blue) produce daily and monthly estimates of a of broad-scale climate parameters. BCE models (light green) are commonly used for species-level analysis and are often used to estimate distribution over a wide area. Process based models (light green) usually involve plant functional groups and use physiological processes to estimate distribution of groups across a wide spatial scale. Successional models (light green) are oriented toward patch-level interactions. The spatial extent of frameworks and indices (yellow) is typically defined by the user's objectives. Hydrological models (blue) can focus on the entire reach of a target river or, more commonly, on a watershed of interest. Most methods focus on estimating conditions over the next century and few address seasonal variations. Exceptions include hydrological models, process-based models, and some index-based methods.

provided a review of aquatic assessments as well as assessment modeling methods. In-stream flow modeling is a habitat-based method that describes a natural environmental regime, which can be used to assess the extent of hydrologic alteration resulting from climate change (Meyers and others 1999). Models that estimate nutrient uptake and hydrodynamic properties (nutrient spiraling model) quantify the simultaneous processes of nutrient cycling by biota and downstream transport of nutrients by water flow. This can be translated to measure of biological productivity or nutrient retentiveness through the use of bioenergetic models. Bioenergetic models are also used to estimate the growth rate of fish and other organisms as well as the effects of changing temperature regimes. Food web models allow user to analyze the indirect effects of climate change through observed changes in food web interactions. For instance, loss of fish because of extreme temperatures or of algae due to anthropogenic disturbance has cascading effects on river and lake systems (Meyers and others 1999). Watershed-level vulnerability assessments (e.g., Fig. 3.2), which integrate information from multiple sources, are very useful from a management perspective, and recent advances in methodologies have been published (USDA 2011; Furniss and others 2012).

3.2.2 Adaptive Capacity Models

This category covers a variety of methods that focus on aspects of adaptive capacity, which often can be directly translated into vulnerability (Tables 3.1, 3.2). Adaptive capacity can apply to resources at a variety of scales. For example, plant communities at ecotones are often considered to be less resilient or to have limited adaptive capacity because of their occurrence in a narrow band of environmental conditions (Allen and Breshears 1998). Greater species diversity has been suggested as an ecosystem characteristic incurring greater resilience to climate change because of functional redundancy, overlap, and connectivity (Peterson and others 1998). Because adaptive capacity can directly tie to genetic diversity and adaptation through natural selection, species-level models of adaptive capacity are common applications. Species dispersal ability (e.g., Cushman and others 2011), species range (Thomas and others 2004), thermal tolerance (Sinervo and others 2010), bioenergetics, and other variables have been used to measure the adaptive capacity of species to deal with changing conditions. Models within this category are useful in that they often consider density, extinction rates, and similar variables rather than focusing on presence-absence (Buckley 2008). However, these methods rely on a certain degree of information regarding species physiological processes and, in many cases, demographic data. Adaptive capacity models are often limited by available data; for example, some species may contain unexpressed genetic variation that would permit adaptation to novel climate conditions such as increased temperatures or dryness, but such information is often not available to researchers and managers (Davis and Shaw 2001).

Processes such as survival, growth, reproduction, and dispersal may change stochastically (e.g., weather-related fluctuations in survival rates) or deterministically (e.g., temporal trends in average survival rates because of climate change) and inform how species may be vulnerable to climate change. In one example of a study of an adaptive capacity, Kearney and others (2009) integrated biophysical models and evolutionary theory to predict climate affects for future habitat suitability of mosquitoes as well as traits such as egg resistance to desiccation, which is known to limit dispersal. Interestingly, the potential habitat of the mosquito was predicted to increase due to warming trends, although water availability might continue to be limited in some regions. The authors found evidence that the mosquito may

Table 3.2. Best use, strengths, and weaknesses of analyses commonly used for predicting future conditions. All methods require climate inputs such as future temperature and precipitation but vary in how data is processed to determine vulnerability. At the most flexible, natural history data on species traits is sufficient for many index based measuring methods. More intensive analyses require detailed data on CO_2 uptake and nutrient cycling obtained from experimental data. All methods are sensitive to bias and uncertainties in climate data.

Analysis type	Input	Output	Best use	Ease of use	Strength	Weakness
Hydrological Models	Climate data Observational data	Flow volume Flow timing Evaporation rates	Generate important data on water availability Watershed analysis	Ranges from moderate to highly intensive model application requiring trained users	Highly quantitative, provides estimate of future condition	Sensitive to bias and uncertainties in climate data and model assumptions
Adaptive Capacity Models	Climate data Experimental data	Survivorship Extinction risk Energetic cost/output	Species-level assessments Biodiversity studies	Ranges from easily applied to more intensive methods requiring trained researcher	Good precision; able to estimate thresholds of tolerances; actual measures of population change	Typically very specific to study organism; can require considerable data input; often consider a limited number of exposure sources (e.g., temperature only)
Bioclimate Envelope (BCE)	Climate data Species/habitat presence data	Estimate of spatial distribution of future suitable climates	Species/biome-level assessments Biodiversity	Requires knowledge of and access to statistical modeling programs	Quick process; can be generated from wide range of data; can be applied to multiple biological scales	Best for large geographic areas; cannot infer future novel communities; not a stand-alone measure of vulnerability
Successional Models	Climate data Physiological process data Disturbance data	Successional stage Biomass and structure information	Individuals Plant functional groups Plant communities	Requires knowledge of and access to specific software programs	Quantitative; estimates future conditions, includes multiple processes	Limited to one level of biological diversity; not a stand-alone measure of vulnerability
Integrated Models	Climate data Disturbance data	Future distribution of target Future condition of vegetation structure and biomass Future disturbance regimes	Typically higher levels of organization (e.g., plant functional groups)	Requires highly specialized knowledge and access to specific software programs. Integrates multiple distinct modeling methods.	Information on multiple interacting impacts; may include some measures of sensitivity and adaptive capacity	Requires considerable data input
Frameworks	Stakeholder/ expert opinion Scientific data/ literature	Relative vulnerability Priority areas or tasks	Specific management targets (e.g., species or habitats of concern)	Minimal modeling skills needed. Often employs facilitated workshops.	Flexible and solution driven	Data are qualitative and subject to bias of user
Indices	Climate data Expert opinion Experimental data	Relative vulnerability	Species Habitats	Can compare vulnerability of a diversity of targets. Individual or group implementation.	Flexible and directly relates to management intervention points.	Output is qualitative and subject to bias of stakeholder

USDA Forest Service RMRS-GTR-309. 2013.

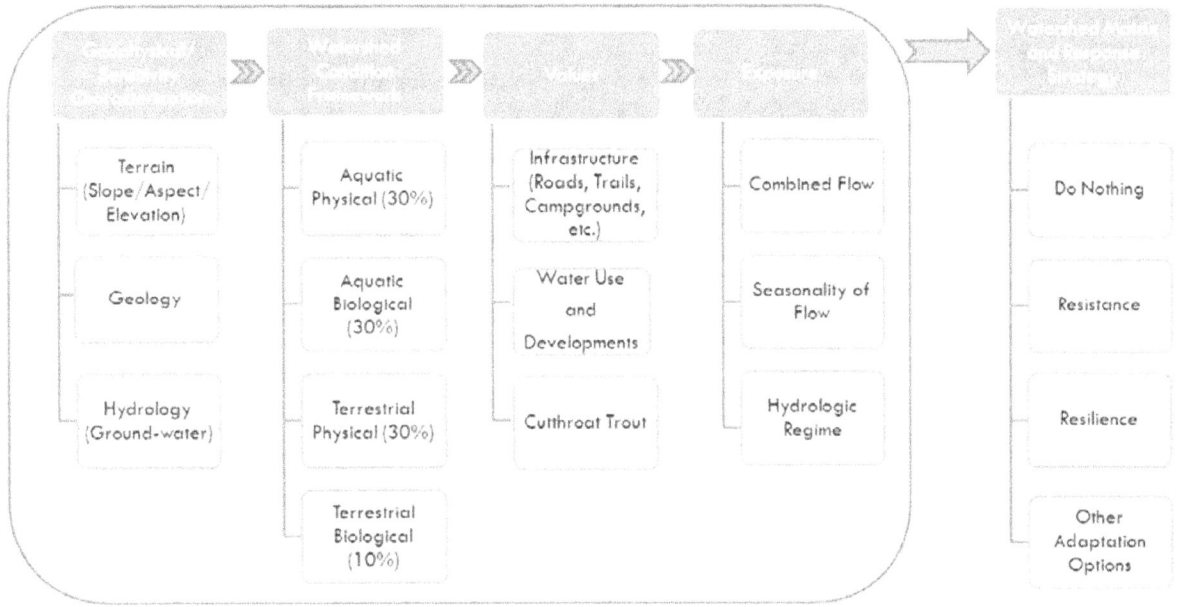

Figure 3.2. Example of the Gallatin National Forest watershed vulnerability model (from Louie 2012).

develop increased resistance to egg desiccation under climate change, highlighting the relatively understudied impact of warming trends on accelerating evolutionary change in ectothermic animals.

The ability of species and natural communities to shift geographically in conjunction with shifting climates is an important aspect of adaptive capacity. Landscape analyses that identify species immigration patterns under future conditions give managers insight as to how individual species will respond to climate change, and are often used to generate estimates of species (or habitat) vulnerability. Cushman and others (2011) specifically address species' sensitivity to landscape fragmentation and future expectations for landscape change due to warming trends to identify species and areas most in need of habitat restoration or relocation measures. In another example, the model SHIFT is used to simulate tree seed dispersal and potential colonization under climate change based on factors of distance and abundance (Iverson and others 2004).

In the absence of genotype changes or dispersal, the current adaptive capacity of a species or population depends on local factors related to survival and reproduction. Dynamic bioenergetic models link a bioenergetic or biophysical model with other models of species traits to estimate changes to survival or reproduction under climate change. Analyses that link demographic models of population and metapopulation dynamics can incorporate processes of survival, growth, reproduction and dispersal into estimates of extinction risk (Akçakaya 2009). For example, Sinervo and others (2010) analyzed extinction risk in lizards in Mexico by estimating activity time during reproduction and timing of breeding to assess adaptations that affect thermal extinctions. In their study, Sinervo and others (2010) describe widespread declines of lizards across four continents and within tropical, temperate, rainforest, and desert habitats. Their analysis, showed that climate change could compromise population growth rates to the degree that local extinction rates will approach 20% by 2080. Meyers (2001) discusses the application of these types of models to fish communities.

3.2.3 Distribution Models

Distribution models are used to estimate future habitat suitability or species distributions given projections for changes in climate conditions. These models are based on the relationship between species distribution and climate or other environmental variables (Pearson and others 2003). For this discussion, we group species distribution models into four primary categories: environmental envelope models, process or simulation based models, succession models, and integrated models (Appendix 1).

Environmental envelope and process based models are able to analyze individual species and higher levels of organization but do not necessarily provide estimates of abundance (as compared to adaptive capacity models). Succession or Forest gap models are able to provide estimates of abundance but primarily focus on changes to species assemblages for a particular landscape. Integrated models represent an expanding diversity of models that incorporate elements of the other three categories of models and sometimes include adaptive capacity. These methods differ in their use of temporal variability: where bioclimate envelopes tend to estimate future suitable habitat or conditions at predefined points in time, process-based models are often able incorporate and output rates of change or generate estimates of change over time.

There are a number of assumptions common to both environmental envelope and process-based models (from Hansen and others 2001 and others):

- Climate-species relationships will remain constant over time.
- Both correlative (climate envelope) and more mechanistic models tend to ignore dispersal and species interactions (McMahon and others 2011). Dispersal or tracking to new suitable climates will be unhindered by other factors. In reality, communities may experience barriers and transitions may lag where long-lived species persist many decades.
- Many modeling techniques use mean temperature or precipitation values, which assumes that changes in averages over time will be as or more important than changes in extreme weather events and short-term variability patterns (Gonzales and others 2010). Depending upon the organisms studied, this may not be a valid assumption.
- Many studies do not consider the timing or seasonality of changes, which may be more important than averages.

Environmental envelope models

The first group of distribution models, environmental envelope models, encompasses a variety of different statistical approaches to describe the relationship between species/biome/habitat presence and climate and, sometimes, other variables (Box 3.1; Appendix 1). This family of models is based on species niche theory, which views the niche as an evolved characteristic comprising the total range of multiple factors that determine where a species can maintain a positive population growth rate over time (Hutchinson 1957; Chase and Liebold 2003; Colwell and Rangel 2009). An example is **bioclimate envelope** (BCE) models, which are applied to both plant and animal species. A large proportion of studies used in vulnerability assessments incorporate BCE models to predict the effect of climate change on species distributions (Parmesan and Yohe 2003; Pearson and others 2003; Rehfeldt and others 2006; Chen and others 2011; Notaro and others 2012). Estimates of the degree or magnitude of shifts in distribution are used to identify species or habitats that are likely to experience the greatest negative

Box 3.1. Statistical and non-statistical approaches for estimating the relationship between climate and species, habitats, or biodiversity.

- **Regression Methods (General Linear Models (GLM), regression trees).** Describes the influence of numerous predictors (climate conditions) on a variable of interest (presence, mortality). Results often form the basis of maps that represent spatial influence of predictors. Example: DISTRIB (Iverson and Prasad 1998 or Iverson and others 1999a). These models project distribution of tree species and aggregate results to present changes in community type. Projections are modeled from the current relationships between tree presence and climate and soil characteristics. Physiological data are not required, which allows for its application to a large number of species. However, these models are not able to integrate the effects of competition, CO_2, or dispersal (though Iverson and others [1999] have developed a model that considers dispersal ability) and establishment capacities. Like many such approaches, these models also assume that the relationship between environment and species will remain constant over time.
    - **Bagging Trees**—Similar to above but uses resampling technique to reduce error. Species that are not well described by predictors will show large variation in output trees, indicating uncertainty.
    - **Multivariate Adaptive Regression**—Splines are used for analysis of continuous variables, which are effectively partitioned into intervals. Example: Rehfeldt and others 1999.
    - **Mahalanobis Distance (MD)**—Multivariate technique. Defines perpendicular major and minor axes and then calculates distance from centroid in n-dimensional space based on covariance of axes lengths. Allows user to consider relative influence of predictor variables. Example: Bradley 2009.
    - **Random Forest**—Classification system that produces robust estimates of species presence. Used in Rehfeldt and others 2006.
    - **Multiple regression models**—Example: Energy theory (Biodiversity). Currie (2001) related biodiversity of a broad spectrum of organisms to spatial patterns of summer and winter precipitation and temperatures using multiple regression. Methods assume that the relationship between biodiversity and climate will remain constant.
- **Machine learning methods (non-statistical) (Artificial Neural Networks, genetic algorithms [GA], GARP, classification analysis and decision tree [CART])**—A group of methods that use algorithms to allow computers to "learn" from experience and improve performance over time. Output is generally in the form of if-then and do not rely on assumptions of relationships between the environment and species suitability. An example is presented in Termansen and others 2006.
- **Cellular Automata**—Used to predict succession, spread of invasive species, plant migration, and, in MigClim, species distribution. This analysis predicts the status of cells over time according to rules about influences of adjacent cells.

Box 3.1. Statistical and non-statistical approaches for estimating the relationship between climate and species, habitats, or biodiversity.

impact due to projected climate effects. Because these analyses focus around climate mediated patterns of distribution, they are best used to predict changes in distribution over large scales where climate is a primary driver. However, within this, the physical range can be quite flexible (see Appendix 1: Table 3.2)

There are a number of advantages and disadvantages of BCE models for estimating response to climate change. BCE models are useful in that they can provide data on species presence or absence with relatively general input data (e.g., Notaro and others 2012: Table 3.2). However, BCE models are less effective for predicting species extinctions because they do not incorporate measures of actual population dynamics (Buckley 2008) or adaptive potential. They also cannot reliably predict shifts in species distribution at small spatial scales. However, new methods are continually being developed to incorporate factors such as dispersal (e.g., Iverson and others 2008; Cushman and others 2010). There may also be problems where models assume species' realized niche, the niche space that a species occupies when other factors such as competition and ability to reach suitable habitat are taken into account, can be adequately described by climate variables (Colwell and Rangel 2009). Similarly, BCE models assume species are in equilibrium with their environment, which may limit the capacity of some models to generate realistic predictions of future range shifts. Further, analyses may assume that current locations of species represent environmental conditions suitable for all life history stages (seedlings and adult trees for instance), which, if incorrect, may overestimate suitability when used to predict future site potential (Falk, in press). Many of these issues are being addressed by combining results generated from BCE models with other methods that can measure non-climate impacts (see Appendix 1 for examples). Indeed, one advantage of BCE models is that they appear to be readily integrated into synthetic approaches for estimating species response (e.g., Iverson and others 2004, 2008; Davison and others 2012).

By combining projections for several species, BCE analyses are also able to generate data regarding biodiversity. In some instances, BCE analysis has been applied directly to estimates of species richness (e.g., Currie 2001). However, relationships between species richness and temperature and precipitation tend to be nonlinear, and, given that predicted changes often fall outside of observed ranges, extrapolation of richness patterns or other diversity measures may not accurately predict future change (Currie 2001). Still, BCE models provide a powerful tool for estimating future loss or potential degree of changing in suitable habitats (Heikkinen and others 2006). Estimating the impact of global change on aggregate indices of biodiversity through analysis with BCE models has many applications for large scale assessments of climate impacts (Currie 2001; Notaro and others 2012). Estimating biodiversity or species richness is particularly useful for identifying hotspots of vulnerability and potentially important areas for prioritized conservation action. Where information is limited regarding factors that influence species range, BCE models remain a good way to estimate climate change effects on biodiversity and may provide more precise estimates of future effects than species assemblage models (Heikkinen and others 2006).

Process-based or simulation models

The second group of models includes **process-based** or **simulation** models, which simulate ecosystem processes by creating mathematical representations of biological and physical processes. A large number of process-based or simulation type models focus on vegetation, which is often defined by a type or by dominant life forms. Thus, output of process-based analyses is commonly generated at higher levels of organization like biome or ecosystem. Since these types of models examine a much more fundamental aspect of ecosystems, they tend to be more responsive to environmental changes such as climate (Swantson and others 2011). These models may also incorporate important elements that have influence at smaller scales. These models range in complexity from **biogeographic** (equilibrium) model that require only long-term average climate and use biogeographic rules to determine vegetation type and density, to the more complicated successional models that simulate dynamic changes based on biogeochemical processes. Biogeochemical models are valuable because they incorporate dynamic climate variables as well as a high degree of interaction among variables to simulate important processes over time and space (Feenstra 2009). They can provide results relevant to biodiversity-focused assessments, including the functional and structure characteristics of the modeled community. However, biogeochemical models do not directly determine what vegetation is likely to exist at a given location.

Dynamic global vegetation models (DGVMs) combine biogeographic and biogeochemical model methods to model the response of broader plant functional groups or community types (Bachelet and others 2001; Notaro and others 2012; Table 3.1, Appendix 1). DGVMs can incorporate disturbance, ecophysiological processes, soil and litter dynamics, and hydrologic variables to simulate vegetation response. Vegetation response is based upon the dynamic feedback of biochemical processes on vegetation distribution (Peng 2000) Importantly, DGVMs also include carbon fertilization effects, which might reduce the impact of warming on plant distribution change and is an issue not addressed by BCE models. Many DGVMs also model carbon cycling (sinks, sources, and fluxes), an important element in climate-biosystem feedbacks (Moritz and others 2012). Though they do not estimate distributions of individual species, DGVMs can incorporate competitive effects by simulating changes in cover (biomass and NPP) and distribution of plant functional types.

Successional models (e.g., JABOWA, Forest Gap Models) are a class of process based models (also called dynamic biogeographical model, Peng 2000) used for studying communities by simulating the influence of growth, ecophysiology, disturbance, and species interactions on composition, biomass, and structure over time (Tables 3.1, 3.2). Forest Gap models are typically individual based models, i.e., they simulate population and community dynamics based on the modeled response of individual organisms (e.g., trees or shrubs). Species distributions are determined at larger scales in modeling by the dominant influence of climate and at smaller scales by a variety of influences. Unlike other model methods, this group is able to output estimates of plant cover, composition, and relative abundance at relatively fine spatial scales (e.g., individual trees and stands). Like other models, successional models tend to focus on plant communities, although these results can be fed into habitat suitability models for animals and other biota.

An equivalent approach on the animal side is the **ecophysical** model, which estimates potential activity hours and food requirements to meet certain energetic costs (Buckley 2008). When data are available, these can be coupled with population dynamic models to create dynamic bioenergetic models (see adaptive capacity model discussion) from which species range can be predicted (e.g., Buckley 2008). However, these models, as with most process based studies, are only as good as the empirical data upon which they are based and are often computationally intense.

Integrated modeling methods

Analysis, especially those that attempt to inform multi-scale perspectives, must take into account both large-scale, climate-driven patterns in biodiversity as well as more local-scale processes relating to species interactions and disturbance regimes. In recognition of this and in an attempt to address shortcomings in species distribution models, a number of efforts have combined methods to improve the accuracy of predictions as well as generate more biologically meaningful data. This group, referred to here as integrated modeling methods, represents a growing body of analyses methods used to inform vulnerability or impact assessments (Table 3.1; Appendix 1). Some examples are:

- Buckley (2008) linked population dynamics and energetics/biophysical models to estimate population growth as a function of activity hours. The authors then integrate individual energetic and population dynamic models with spatial environmental data to predict distribution and abundance of vertebrate and plant species.

- MigClim (Engler and Guisan 2009; Appendix 1) is a recently developed program that couples predictive distribution maps, representing a species' habitat suitability as a function of evolving climate, with a cellular automaton that simulates adaptive capacity relating to dispersal, colonization, growth, and extinction of the species in the landscape under differing conditions. This model runs in ArcGIS to simulate plant dispersal under climate change and landscape fragmentation scenarios and, used in conjunction with envelope type analysis (requires maps of current and future suitable habitat distributions), gives a spatially explicit prediction that can be used to assess species vulnerability.

- Iverson and others (2008) combined bioclimate distribution analyses with a model for species dispersal and a qualitative system for identifying the relative influence of species traits (modification factors or MODFAC) that accounts for climate and non-climate-related response variables for tree species in the eastern United States. This analysis produces an estimate of species ranges under future conditions.

- Barrio and others (2006) described a process that integrates four models in a scale-dependent hierarchical framework to study the impacts of climate and land use change scenarios on species' distributions at fine resolutions. This method combines two distribution models: SPECIES, a continental scale bioclimatic envelope model and downscaled SPECIES, a regional-scale bioclimate and land use suitability model; a dispersal model; and ALCOR, a connectivity model. SPECIES is a model that employs an artificial neural network (ANN) to define BCE based on inputs generated through a climate-hydrological linked process model. Applied to systems in the United Kingdom and Spain, this analysis was able to attribute specific patterns of landscape change to climate change. Specifically, increased fragmentation in landscapes derived from the development of gaps within existing habitat structure rather than shifts in habitat zonal types.

- LANDFIRE uses spatially explicit modeling of dynamic interactions between vegetation, climate and disturbance to create probabilities regarding future conditions. These probabilities represent departure from preset reference conditions (see Chapter 4.1) and vulnerability is represented as future departure from norm (e.g., Baker 1989; Keane and others 2006; Mladenoff 2004; used in LandFire Project to compute FRCC).

- FireBGCv2 is a simulation modeling platform that merges a Gap model (FIRESUM); a mechanistic vegetation succession model (BIOME-BGC); a spatially explicit fire model (FARSITE) incorporating ignition, spread, and effects on ecosystem components; and a detailed fuel treatment module (FIRESUM, Keane and others 2011). FireBGCv2 dynamically simulates synergistic and interacting effects of weather and climatology, vegetation growth and succession, disturbance (e.g., wildfire and bark beetles), and land management (e.g., prescribed fire and thinning) on landscape structure and ecosystem processes.

3.2.4 Prioritization Methods

Indices

Indices are generally suitable for questions that explore biological diversity in the aggregate since they provide a ranking or relative measure of vulnerability among a group of species (Feenstra and others 1998) or in cases where multiple datasets are

Table 3.3. Examples of methods used to provide relative measures of vulnerability or identify areas of vulnerability. Type refers to the method employed. Quantifications typically tally traits associated with vulnerability. Models typically combine some type of tallying method and extrapolate it to spatially explicit issues (e.g., landscape fragmentation).

Name	Scale	Type	Description	Target	Available from
NatureServe's Climate Change Vulnerability Index for species (CCVI) and habitats (HCCVI)	Global-fixed; range of species or habitats	Quantification	CCVI consists of ranking system that considers spatial estimates of exposure and species traits indicative of sensitivity and adaptive capacity and categorizes species according to their level of vulnerability. HCCVI uses results of CCVI as well as estimates of habitat change, including disturbance effects, to rank habitat vulnerability.	Animal and plant species and habitats	www.natureserve.org/prodServices/climatechange/ClimateChange.jsp
System for Assessing Vulnerability of Species (SAVS)	Flexible	Quantification	Scoring system based upon 22 traits predictive of species vulnerability to climate change. Produces value used to compare relative vulnerability among species.	Terrestrial vertebrate species	http://www.fs.fed.us/rm/grassland shrubland-desert/products/species vulnerability/
Environmental Protection Agency Framework	Flexible	Quantification	Framework for categorizing the relative vulnerability of threatened and endangered species to climate change. Forms a matrix that simultaneously considers species vulnerability to ongoing population declines and future negative impacts from climate change. Aims to focus management actions.	Threatened and endangered species	EPA/600/R-09/01
Water Supply Stress Index Model(WaSSI)	Flexible	Quantification	Models local watershed stress by comparing water supply and demand in a particular area.	Water	http://www.fs.fed.us/ccrc/tools/wassi.shtml
Vulnerability Surface	Flexible	Model	Uses a three-dimensional analytical surface to determine relative vulnerability. Applicable to variety of systems. Amendable to targets that are not easily described by mathematics.	Animals	Luers 2005; Luers and others 2003
Forest Tree Genetic Risk Assessment System (ForGRAS)	Flexible	Model/ Quantification	Creates a vulnerability index from four different measures of future expected change in species distribution. Rates species according to intrinsic attributes and external threats that influence species vulnerability to climate change.	Plants	Potter and Crane 2010

combined (Sullivan and Meigh 2005). Indices are often applied at scales ranging from management unit to regional or subregional levels (Table 3.3). Alternatively, an index might be applied across a species' range (e.g., NatureServe). These methods are relatively easy to compute and are flexible to a diversity of input type but may reflect more generalized relationships at the cost of accurate predictions (Table 3.2). Variables used in such indices are often given equal weight, which can provide misleading results where individual species have particular overriding influences. Still, indices, unlike many of the mathematical modeling approaches discussed earlier, can be constructed to measure aspects of vulnerability directly and can be used alone to generate climate change vulnerability assessments (e.g., Coe and others 2012; Bagne and Finch 2012). Two primary approaches are used to generate scores: Quantification of traits considered important predictors of species sensitivity and adaptive capacity (e.g., SAVS, NatureServe's Climate Change Vulnerability Index, and NCCVI) and methods that model vulnerability based upon predetermined schemes that categorize relative impact and response (e.g., Luers 2005).

Many of the systems listed in Table 3.3 were developed in direct response to the recognition of the need for specific measures of species and ecosystem vulnerability to climate change. As such, they are tailored to help managers and conservationists identify critical elements, whether species or species trait, most vulnerable to future, expected conditions. The specific nature of these systems, which relates directly to the goal of understanding climate change impacts, lends them considerable weight for addressing vulnerability assessment needs. In addition, many of these scoring systems use data generated from distribution models or otherwise build upon data regarding future expected conditions. Therefore, indices represent a synthetic product based on data from a variety of sources. However, as such, many of these systems are only as good as the data used to generate a score, and a well-developed application of a scoring system can be quite labor intensive. In addition, though very good at focusing the user's attention toward climate impacts, these tools often do not incorporate other interacting stressors and require additional and separate analyses to create comprehensive management strategies. Future developments are likely to integrate additional methods into the scoring process to create new approaches that can simultaneously consider multiple stressors as well as distinguish vulnerability across a landscape.

Frameworks

Frameworks (Table 3.4) are similar to indices in that they provide a relative measure of vulnerability. However, they are often focused on targets that are not easily described by mathematical relationships and commonly have a socio-economic focus. Where indices use scores to quantify vulnerability, frameworks are generally based around the identification of targets and hazards and employ an algorithm to relate vulnerability to sensitivity and exposure divided by conditions that ameliorate negative impacts on the target (exceeds threshold, e.g., Leurs 2005; adaptive capacity, e.g., Fontaine and Steinemann 2009). Targets and hazards are often defined by consensus of opinions or responses generated by interviews or facilitated workshops. As such, frameworks are not necessarily a method for measuring vulnerability so much as a tool to identify vulnerabilities within a system of interest.

Fontaine and Steinemann (2009) presented a simple framework and algorithm to assess vulnerability for social sectors that could be applied to natural systems as well. In their system, each element, exposure, sensitivity, and adaptive capacity, is considered on a 1-5 Likert scale (psychometric commonly used in research

Table 3.4. Examples of frameworks that can be used to create or organize climate change vulnerability assessments.

Name/source	Description	Target	Available from:
Czúcz and others 2009	Framework consists of adaptive capacity indicators that account for primary coping options or mechanisms. These indicators are quantified using landscape indices based on quality and distribution of habitat patches, exposure estimates based on GCM outputs under various conditions, and estimates of sensitivity (four categories or types are identified). Produces climate vulnerability maps.	Natural resources	Czúcz and others 2009
Ford and Smit 2004	A framework for assessing the vulnerability of communities in the Canadian Artic to risks associated with climate change.	Canadian Arctic Region	Ford and Smit 2004
Environmental risk assessment/ management framework for climate change impact assessments	Though not explicitly a vulnerability assessment, this framework addresses sensitivity, exposure, and adaptive capacity components. Uses risk analysis methods identified in IPCC technical guidelines to assess climate impacts and adaptations within a framework that incorporates stakeholders. Identifies thresholds that are then used for assessment.	U.S.	http://www.epa.gov/ncea/global/approaches.htm
Vulnerability Assessment Method (VAM)	Acquires data from stakeholders (experts) to assess hazard and causes of vulnerability by quantifying through a simple algorithm level of effect of future natural hazard on exposure, sensitivity, and adaptive capacity.	Social sector but other applications possible	Fontaine and Steinemann 2009
A multidisciplinary, multi-scale framework for assessing vulnerabilities to global change (ATEAM project)	Framework for combining several types and versions of assessments regarding problem target. Based upon comprehensive algorithm framework that combines elements of traditional climate change vulnerability assessments, with adaptation and impact assessments. Also has elements of risk assessment (risk of alternate scenario). Combines ecosystem, economic, and social sectors.	Ecosystems and ecosystem services	Metzger and others 2005
EPA's Regional Vulnerability Assessment (ReVA) Program	Designed to develop and demonstrate approaches that address phases of ecological risk assessment that focus on integrating and synthesizing information on the spatial patterns of multiple exposure to allow a comparison and prioritization of risks. Combines elements of vulnerability and risk assessments.	Natural resources	Smith and others 2005
Assessing Climate Change Effects on Land Use and Ecosystems: from Regional Analysis to the European Scale (ACCELERATES)	Created climate change scenarios based on the ATEAM project. Integrates land use data, species distribution, and habitat fragmentation within a common scenario framework to synthesize impacts for different global change problems.	Natural resources	Roundsevell and others 2006

questionnaires) representing very low to extreme likelihood of effect. In a case study of drought in Washington State, this scale corresponds to the frequency and severity of drought, where, for instance, the likelihood of frequent droughts could be considered very low, low, moderate, high, or extreme. Fontaine and Steinemann (2009) used stakeholder (various water users) interviews to populate their dataset. Vulnerability was calculated according to well recognized equation, $V = (E+S)/A$ (IPCC 2007), where exposure and sensitivity are additive effects leading to vulnerability that is reduced to a lesser or greater degree by adaptive capacity. In this way, Fontaine and Steinmann use knowledge and values of stakeholders to measure vulnerability. Importantly, though this type of method may rely on human interpretation, it is able to quantify and integrate all three elements of vulnerability. To apply this to a natural setting, expert interviews might be substituted for stakeholder provided information.

A more biologically oriented system was presented by Czúcz and others (2009) who developed a framework that consists of adaptive capacity indicators that account for primary coping options or mechanisms. These indicators are quantified using landscape indices based on quality and distribution of habitat patches, exposure estimates based on GCM outputs under various conditions, and estimates of sensitivity (four categories or types are identified). Ultimately, this process produces climate vulnerability maps.

3.3 Issues in Predicting Response

It is critical to understand how response measures relate to vulnerability to best identify strategies that prepare for and cope with climate change (see Chapter 1, Figure 1.2). As part of the assessment process, we must understand how well measures of response represent the range of potential effects on species, habitats, and ecosystems. However, the complexity of biological systems prevents a perfect representation by any one or combination of methods. Only through a careful consideration of biological complexities can we identify strengths and weaknesses in various approaches as well as provide insight into best management practices.

3.3.1 Critical Thresholds, Ecosystem Tipping Points, and Other Considerations

As discussed in section 3.2, many studies predict changes in species distributions in response to changing climate (e.g., Rehfeldt and others 2006; Notaro and others 2012). At local scales, community composition reflects changes in the suitability of existing habitat for species persistence. Both modeling and empirical studies suggest that such changes due to climate alone are likely to be expressed at multi-annual to decadal time scales (Allen and Breshears 1998; Parmesan and Yohe 2003; Chen and others 2011). In contrast, severe, large-scale disturbances can reorganize ecosystems mass and energy on much shorter time scales of days to months (Overpeck and others 1990; Falk, in press). In many cases it may be combinations of climate change and severe disturbance that is most likely to trigger abrupt ecosystem transitions into novel configurations, rather than either factor acting separately.

Following major disturbances that occur during periods of climate stress, ecosystems may recover not into the pre-disturbance conditions but into novel community types. For example, conversion of pine-dominated communities to dominance by Gambel oak (*Quercus gambellii*), New Mexico locust (*Robinia Neomexicana*), and interior chaparral species is frequently observed in the Southwest following major fires (Savage and Mast 2005). These new configurations can be resilient in their new state and resistant to return to pre-disturbance conditions (Kitzberger and others 2011). In addition to ecological effects, these transitions also include potentially persistent alterations to geomorphic, soil, hydrological, and biogeochemical systems (Scheffer and others 2001). Such abrupt transitions are predicted to become more common under conditions of altered future climate and amplified disturbance regimes (Flannigan and others 2000; Westerling and others 2006; Zinck and others 2011).

Abrupt ecological change is generally defined as a threshold response in key biotic and abiotic parameters and ecosystem components (Anderson and others 2008). Such changes may be expressed in shifts in dominant vegetation physiognomy (for example, from forest to shrub communities), especially if established individuals of dominant species do not survive a disturbance event. Altered soil, hydrologic, and biogeochemical conditions can reinforce shifts in vegetation types and disturbance regimes, such as a transition from a low-severity forest surface fire regime to a high-severity chaparral shrubland regime (Mayer 2011). Climate provides the envelope within which these dynamics occur; disturbance provides the trigger for abrupt system reorganization.

A variety of mechanisms may contribute to rapid or even abrupt post-fire ecosystem change under current and near-term climate. First, by definition, severe disturbances such as wildfires leave relatively few surviving established individuals, opening up niche and physical space for community level turnover. This mechanism operates by differential mortality among species, which may relate in turn to life histories adapted to low- or high-severity fire respectively. Second, early post-fire successional pathways may produce different post-fire communities by processes of community assembly, including dispersal distances, order of arrival (or, in the case of sprouting species, vegetative response), tolerance of harsh post-fire physical conditions, competitive ability, and other factors. Third, even where pre-fire community members are present, altered climate conditions may not include climate space suitable for regeneration of previously dominant species, even when these species were able to persist pre-fire as established individuals (Breshears and others 2005). The recruitment niche for many Southwestern species is concentrated in the cooler, wetter region of the species tolerance space as established adults, and during extended drought periods these climate conditions may not occur during recruitment season (Notaro and others 2012). Finally, altered landscape structure (such as anomalously large high-severity patches) following extreme disturbance events (such as anomalously large high-severity patches) may restrict establishment where distance to seed source exceeds the scale of propagule dispersal of previously dominant species, while favoring other species with rapid long-range dispersal.

The collective effect of these disturbance-climate interactions can be to rapidly and persistently change landscape patterns and processes including disturbance regimes, vegetation composition, carbon dynamics, and hydrologic balance (Lentile and others 2007). At broad spatial scales these changes may constitute a feedback mechanism to the climate system through changes in surface albedo and vegetation productivity. Together with an altered climate envelope, these mechanisms may limit recruitment of previously dominant species while favoring establishment of a different suite of species better adapted to new conditions (Bachelet and others 2001; Loehman and others 2011). Once established, the new community may support novel disturbance regimes that then further exclude prior dominants.

3.3.2 Interactive Effects

No species exists in complete isolation from others. These interactions can be adverse to a given organism (e.g., competitive exclusion, resource competition, disease interactions, and parasitism), leading to reduced population growth rates or local abundance. Species interactions may also be beneficial or even essential, as in the case of mycorrhizal associations between plants and fungi, or dispersal and pollination agents for plants. Thus, a complete assessment of species climate vulnerability needs to include the sensitivity and exposure to alterations in these critical species interactions.

An example of climate-driven vulnerability that is amplified by species interactions involves changes in the phenology (seasonal timing) of plants and their pollinators. Abundant evidence has been compiled of changes in phenology as one of the most pervasive ecological responses to climate change (Walther and others 2002; Weltzin and others 2001; Parmesan 2006).This includes the timing of migrational movements as well as timing of seasonal life cycles. Plants and their herbivores (e.g., insect larvae who use them as food plants) and pollinators rely on being present at the correct relative time in the annual cycle; for example, plants that produce nectar must be in flower to provide the energy source required by hummingbirds and for insects such as bees that gather pollen. Conversely, plant species that rely on particular agents for cross pollination must be ready with mature flowers when those agents are present. Several cases have now been documented of amplified vulnerability of a target species due to climate-driven asynchrony with essential symbionts or mutualists (e.g., Parmesan and others 2003).

A different form of interaction is the amplification of negative impacts of climate change with other ecological processes or agents. For example, in many forests throughout western North America, climate change is interacting with fire and biotic responses such as defoliating insects or bark beetles, in some cases leading to accelerated local extirpation of species (Smithwick 2008; Hicke and Logan 2009). Betancourt and Swetnam (1993) documented the accelerated decline of pinyon (*Pinus edulis*)in New Mexico during a severe drought in the 1950s; while drought was the overall driver of mortality, bark beetles (*Ips* and *Dendroctonus* spp.) were probably the immediate agents of mortality in many areas. Similar die-offs have been observed in other areas (Allen and Breshears 1998). Extensive mortality of Engelmann spruce (*Picea engelmanii*) has been documented in the Pinaleño Mountains of southeastern Arizona, the ecologically tallest of the Sky

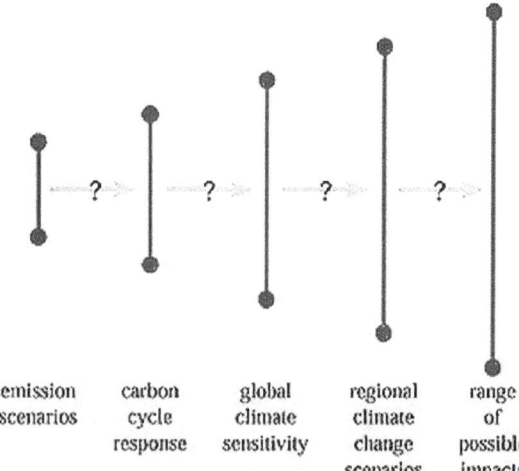

emission scenarios | carbon cycle response | global climate sensitivity | regional climate change scenarios | range of possible impacts

Figure 3.3. From IPCC (2007: 2-2). Range of major uncertainties that are typical in impact assessments, showing the "uncertainty explosion" as these ranges are multiplied to encompass a comprehensive range of future consequences, including physical, economic, social, and political impacts and policy responses (modified after Jones 2000, and "cascading pyramid of uncertainties" in Schneider 1983).

Islands, due to interactions of climate stress, insect outbreaks, and a series of high-severity fires (O'Connor and others 2011). Such interactions of stressors would predict enhanced vulnerability of many species when compared to the effects of climate change alone.

3.3.3 Uncertainty

Models can never perfectly describe the real world and the future can never be known. Thus vulnerability assessments reflect a degree of uncertainty (Fig. 3.3). The key for dealing with uncertainty is to recognize its sources, amplitude, and significance. We have highlighted a number of sources relating to unknown processes within the biological community, but we also need to highlight technical sources of uncertainty. For example, the variability among projections generated by different GCMs can be reduced, or at least bracketed, by using outputs from multiple models (Notaro and others 2012; Quijada-Mascarenas, in review). In one approach, model projections are weighted along a performance scale based upon estimates of past climate conditions (Notaro and others 2012). Variation among GCMs for a given emission scenario (the amount of greenhouse gases, or GHGs, including CO_2 and CH_4) tends to be small relative to the uncertainty associated with projecting future GHG emissions (Nakicenovic and others 2000 in IPCC 2007). Future emissions will be affected by a wide variety of variables globally, including human population growth, regulations, and energy development, and thus are influenced strongly by political and economic forces as well as the degree of social consensus about reducing GHG emissions. Consequently, a best-practice approach for vulnerability assessments has traditionally been to include results under a range of possible emissions scenarios. However, recent studies show that the trajectory of GHG output since emissions scenarios began to be used has consistently exceeded the highest scenarios used by the IPCC, and recorded temperatures are correspondingly at the high end of the range of projections (Smith and others 2009). Vulnerability assessments may be best served when based upon projections of models run under the higher range of emissions.

There is also inherent uncertainty in estimates of vulnerability that rely on incomplete knowledge. Management decisions are limited by available information and the feasibility of measuring vulnerability of the target of interest. For example, experimental observations can be made for sedentary organisms at a small scale (e.g., plants in a patch of prairie) but are less feasible for highly mobile organisms or landscape scale processes, thus, uncertainty is a function of the selected assessment targets. As discussed in previous sections, ecological thresholds and interactive effects are often undefined but likely to have strong influences on species or community response to climate change. Scenario planning is a common approach to coping with uncertainty in climate models where impacts on targets and their vulnerability are assessed across a range of possible climate futures so that robust management options can be identified (Peterson and others 2003). Similarly, multiple response measures (Chapter 4) may be used to estimate vulnerability for a target and identify common sources of sensitivity and exposure (e.g., VEMAP, Notaro and others 2012).

Literature Cited

Akçakaya H.R. 2009. RAMAS GIS: linking spatial data with population viability analysis, Version 6 beta. Setauket, NY: Applied Biomathematics.

Allen, C.D., and D.D. Breshears. 1998. Drought-induced shift of a forest-woodland ecotone: Rapid response to climate variation. Proceedings of the National Academy of Sciences U.S. 95: 14839-14842.

Bachelet, D., J. M. Lenihan, C. Daly, [and others]. 2001. MC1: A dynamic vegetation model for estimating the distribution of vegetation and associated ecosystem fluxes of carbon, nutrients, and water, Version 1.0., US Forest Service, Pacific Northwest Research Station, Gen. Tech. Rep. PNW-GTR-508: 95 pp.

Baker, W. L. 1989. Classification of the riparian vegetation of the montane and subalpine zones in western Colorado. Great Basin Naturalist 49: 214-228.

Barrio G., P.A. Harrison, P.M. Berry, [and others]. 2006. Integrating multiple modeling approaches to predict the potential impacts of climate change on species' distributions in contrasting regions: comparison and implications for policy. Environmental Science and Policy 9: 129-147

Berry, P.M., M.D.A. Roundsevell, P.A. Harrison, and E. Audsley. 2006. Assessing the vulnerability of agricultural land use and species to climate change and the role of policy in facilitating adaptation. Environmental Science and Policy 9: 189-204.

Buckley, L.B. 2008. Linking traits to energetics and population dynamics to predict lizard ranges in changing environments. The American Naturalist 171: E1-E19.

Chase, J. M. and M. A. Leibold 2003. Ecological niches: linking classical and contemporary approaches. University of Chicago Press, Chicago.

Chen, I. C., Hill, J. K., Ohlemüller, R., Roy, D. B., and C. D. Thomas. 2011. Rapid range shifts of species associated with high levels of climate warming. Science 333: 1024-1026.

Colwell R. K., and T. F. Rangel. 2009. Hutchinson's duality: the once and future niche. Proceeding of the National Academy of Science, USA, 106: 651–19 658.

Crookston, N.L., G.E. Rehfeldt, G.E. Dixon, and A.R. Weiskittel. 2010. Addressing climate change in the forest vegetation simulator to assess impacts on landscape forest dynamics. Forest Ecology and Management 260: 1198-1211.

Currie, D. J. 2001. Projected effects of climate change on patterns of vertebrate and tree species richness in the conterminous United States. Ecosystems 4: 216-225.

Cushman, S.A., E.L. Landguth, and C.H. Flather. 2010. Climate change and connectivity: Assessing Landscape and Species Vulnerability. Phase 1. Final Report for the Great Plains Landscape Conservation Cooperative. Available at: http://treesearch.fs.fed.us/pubs/39233

Cushman, S.A., M.J. Chanse, and C. Griffin. 2010. Mapping landscape resistance to identify corridors and barriers for elephant movements in southern Africa. Pages 349-368 in: S. A. Cushman, and F. Heuttman, eds. Spatial complexity, informatics and wildlife conservation. Springer, Tokyo.

Czúcz, B., G. Kröel-Dulay, G. Torda, Z. Molnár, and L. Tõkei. 2009. Regional scale habitat-based vulnerability assessment for the natural ecosystems. IOP Conf. Series: Earth and Environmental Science 6: 442006.

Davison, J.E, S. Coe, D. Finch, [and others]. 2012. Bringing indices of species vulnerability to climate change into geographic space: an assessment across the Coronado National Forest. Biodiversity Conservation 21: 189-204.

Engle, N.L. 2011. Adaptive capacity and its assessment. Global Environmental Change: 647-656.

Engler, R., and A. Guisan. 2009. MIGCLIM: prediction plant distribution and dispersal in a changing climate. Diversity and Distributions 15: 590-601.

Feenstra, J. F., Burton, I. Smith, J.B, and R. S. J. Tol. (eds.) 1998. Handbook on methods for climate change impact assessment and adaptation strategies version 2.0. United Nations Environment Programme, Institute for Environmental Studies.

Fontaine, M., and A.C. Steinemann. 2009. Assessing vulnerability to natural hazards: An impact-based method and application to drought in Washington State. Natural Hazards Review 10:11-18.

Furniss, M. J., K. B. Roby, D. Cenderelli, [and others]. 2012. Assessing the Vulnerability of Watersheds to Climate Change: Results of National Forest Watershed Vulnerability Pilot Assessments. Climate Change Resource Center. U.S. Department of Agriculture, Forest Service 305p. www.fs.fed.us/ccrc/wv.

Gonzalez, P., R. P. Neilson, J. M. Lenihan, R. and J. Drapek. 2010. Global patterns in the vulnerability of ecosystems to vegetation shifts due to climate change. Global Ecology and Biogeography 19: 755–768.

Guertin, D.P., R.H. Fiedler, S.N. Miller, and D.C. Goodrich. 2000. Fuzzy logic for watershed assessment. Proceedings of the ASCE Conference on Science and Technology for the New Millennium: Watershed Management 2000, Fort Collins, CO, June 21-24, 2000.

Gutsche, A., S. Stuart, and E. Turak. 2008. In: J.-C. Vie, C. Hilton-Taylor and S. N. Stuart (eds). The 2008 Review of the IUCN Red List of threatened species. International Union for Conservation of Nature, Gland, Switzerland.

Heikkinen, R. K., Luoto, M., Araújo, [and others]. 2006. Methods and uncertainties in bioclimatic envelope modeling under climate change. Progress in Physical Geography 30: 751-777.

Hicke J.A. and J.A. Logan. 2009. Mapping whitebark pine mortality caused by a mountain pine beetle outbreak with high spatial resolution satellite imagery. International Journal of Remote Sensing 30: 4427-4441.

Hutchinson, G.E. 1957. The multivariate niche. Cold Spring Harbor Symposium. Quantitative Biology 22: 415-421.

Iverson, L.R., M.W. Schwartz, and A.M. Prasad. 2004. How fast and far might tree species migrate in the eastern United States due to climate change? Global Ecology and Biogeography 13: 209-219.

Iverson, L.R., A.M. Prasad, S.N. Matthews, and M. Peters. 2008. Estimating potential habitat for 134 eastern US tree species under six climate scenarios. Forest Ecology and Management 254: 390-406.

Johnson, T., and C. Weaver. 2009. A Framework for Assessing Climate Change Impacts on Water and Watershed Systems. Environmental Management 43: 118-134.

Keane, R.E., L. M. Holsinger, and S.D. Pratt. 2006. Simulating historical landscape dynamics using the landscape fire succession model LANDSUM version 4.0. US Forest Service, Rocky Mountain Research Station. Gen. Tech. Rep. RMRS-GTR-171CD: 73 p.

Keane, Robert E., Rachel A. Loehman, Lisa M. Holsinger. 2011. The FireBGCv2 landscape fire and succession model: a research simulation platform for exploring fire and vegetation dynamics. Gen. Tech. Rep. RMRS-GTR-255. Fort Collins, CO: U.S. Department of Agriculture, Forest Service, Rocky Mountain Research Station. 137 p.

Kearney, M., W.P. Porter, C. Williams, S. Ritchie, and A. Hoffmann. 2009. Integrating biophysical models and evolutionary theory to predict climatic impacts on species' ranges: the dengue mosquito *Aedes aegypti* in Australia. Functional Ecology 23: 528-538.

Keith, D.A., H.R. Akcakaya, W. Thuiller, [and others]. 2008. Predicting extinction risks under climate change: coupling stochastic population models with dynamic bioclimatic habitat models. Biology Letters 4: 560-563.

Lentile, L., P. Morgan, A. Hudak,[and others]. 2007. Post-fire burn severity and vegetation response following eight large wildfires across the western United States. Fire Ecology 3: 91-108.

Leurs, A.L. 2005. The surface of vulnerability: An analytical framework. Global Environmental Change 15: 214-223.

Lischke, H., N.E. Zimmermann, J. Bolliger, S. Rickebusch, and T.J. Loffler. 2006. TreeMig: A forest-landscape model for simulating spatio-temporal patterns from stands to landscape scale. Ecological Modeling 199: 409-420.

Loehman, R.A., J.A. Clark, and R.E. Keane. 2011. Modeling Effects of Climate Change and Fire Management on Western White Pine (*Pinus monticola*) in the Northern Rocky Mountains, USA. Forests 2: 832-860.

Louei, J.Y. 2012. Assessment of Watershed Vulnerability to Climate Change, Gallatin National Forest. In: M. J. Furniss, Roby, K. B., Cenderelli, D.; Chatel, J.; Clifton, C. F.; Clingenpeel, A., and others. 2012. Assessing the Vulnerability of Watersheds to Climate Change: Results of National Forest Watershed Vulnerability Pilot Assessments. Climate Change Resource Center. U.S. Department of Agriculture, Forest Service. 305 p.

Metzger, M.J., R. Leemans, and D. Schröter. 2005. A multidisciplinary multi-scale framework for assessing vulnerabilities to global change. International Journal of Applied Earth Observation and Geoinformation 7: 253-267.

Mladenoff, D.J. 2004. LANDIS and forest landscape models. Ecological Modelling180: 7-19.

Moritz, M. A., Parisien, M. A., Batllori, E., [and others]. 2012. Climate change and disruptions to global fire activity. Ecosphere 3: 49.

Nakicenovic, N., [and others]. 2000. Special Report on Emissions Scenarios: A Special Report of Working Group III of the Intergovernmental Panel on Climate Change, Cambridge University Press, Cambridge, U.K., 599 p. Available at: http://www.grida.no/climate/ipcc/emission/index.htm.

Notaro, M., Mauss, A., and J.W. Williams. 2012. Projected vegetation changes for the American Southwest: combined dynamic modeling and bioclimatic-envelope approach. Ecological Applications 22: 1365-1388.

O'Connor, C. D., G. M. Garfin, [and others]. 2011. "Human Pyrogeography: A New Synergy of Fire, Climate and People is Reshaping Ecosystems across the Globe." Geography Compass 5: 329-350.

Overpeck, J.T., D. Rind, and R. Goldberg. 1990: Climate- induced changes in forest disturbance and vegetation. Nature 343: 51-53

Parmesan C. and G. Yohe. 2003. Globally coherent fingerprints of climate change impacts across natural systems. Nature 421: 37-42.

Parmesan, C. 2006. Ecological and Evolutionary Responses to Recent Climate Change. Annual Review of Ecology, Evolution, and Systematics 37: 637-669.

Pearson, R.G., T.P. Dawson, P.M. Berry, and P.A. Harrison. 2002. Ecological Modeling 154: 289-300.

Peng, C. 2000. From static biogeographical model to dynamic global vegetation model: a global perspective on modelling vegetation dynamics. Ecological Modelling 135: 33-54.

Peterson, Garry, Craig R. Allen, and C.S. Holling. 1998. Ecological Resilience, Biodiversity, and Scale. Nebraska Cooperative Fish and Wildlife Research Unit—Staff Publications. Paper 4.

Peterson, G.D., G.S. Cumming, and S.R. Carpenter. 2003. Scenario Planning: a Tool for Conservation in an Uncertain World. Conservation Biology 17: 358-366.

Rehfeldt, G.E., N.L. Crookston, M.V. Warwell, and J.S. Evans. 2006. Empirical Analyses of Plant-Climate Relationships for the Western United States. International Journal of Plant Sciences 167: 1123-1150.

Rehfeldt, G.E., N.L. Crookston, C. Saenz-Romero, and E.M. Campbell. 2012. North American vegetation model for land-use planning in a changing climate: a solution to large classification problems. Ecological Applications 22: 119-141.

Roundsevell, M.D.A., P.M. Berry, and P.A. Harrison. 2006. Future environmental change impacts on rural land use and biodiversity: a synthesis of the ACCELERATES project. Environmental Science and Policy 9: 93-100.

Savage, M., and J.N. Mast. 2005. How resilient are ponderosa pine ecosystems after crown fires? Canadian Journal of Forest Research 35: 967-977.

Scholes, R.J., S. Linder, and K.M. Siddiqui. 1998. 12. Forests. In: Feenstra, J. F., Burton, I. Smith, J.B, and R. S. J. Tol. (eds.) 1998. Handbook on methods for climate change impact assessment and adaptation strategies version 2.0. United Nations Environment Programme, Institute for Environmental Studies.

Sinervo, B., F. Méndez-de-la-Cruz, D.B. Miles, [and others]. 2010. Erosion of Lizard Diversity by Climate Change and Altered Thermal Niches Science 14: 894-899.

Smith, E.R., L.T. Tran, and R.V. O'Neill. 2005. Regional Vulnerability assessment for the Mid-Atlantic Region: Evaluation of Integration Methods and Assessment Results. U.S Environmental Protection Agency RPT 009LCB04.RPT. 77 p.

Smithwick, E.A.H., M.G. Ryan, D.M. Kashian [and others]. 2008. Modeling the effects of fire and climate change on carbon and nitrogen storage in lodgepole pine (*Pinus contorta*) stands. Global Change Biology 15: 535–548

Steinke, R. 2012. Assessment of Watershed Vulnerability to Climate Change, Coconino National Forest. In: M. J. Furniss, Roby, K. B., Cenderelli, D.; Chatel, J.; Clifton, C. F.; Clingenpeel, A., and others. 2012. Assessing the Vulnerability of Watersheds to Climate Change: Results of National Forest Watershed Vulnerability Pilot Assessments. Climate Change Resource Center. U.S. Department of Agriculture, Forest Service. 305 p.

Sullivan, C.A., and J.R. Meigh. 2005. Targeting attention on local vulnerabilities using an integrated index approach: the example of the climate vulnerability index. Water Science & Technology 51: 69-78.

Thomas, C.D., A. Cameron, R.E., Green, [and others]. 2004. Extinction risk from climate change. Nature 427: 145-148.

Thuiller, W., B. Lafourcade, R. Engler, and M.B. Araújo. 2009. BIOMOD—a platform for ensemble forecasting of species distributions. Ecography 32: 369-373.

Turner, B.L., II, R.E. Kasperson, P.A. Matson, [and others]. 2003. A framework for vulnerability analysis in sustainability science. Proceedings of the National Academy of Sciences 100: 8074-8079.

Walker, P.A., and K.D. Cocks. 1991. HABITAT: A Procedure for Modeling a Disjoint Environmental Envelope for a Plant or Animal Species. Ecology and Biogeography Letters 1: 108 of 108-118.

Walther, G. R., E. Post, P. Convey, [and others]. 2002. Ecological responses to recent climate change. Nature 416: 389-395.

Weltzin, J.F., K.A. Snyder, and D.G. Williams. 2001. Experimental manipulations of precipitation seasonality: effects on oak (*Quercus*) seedling demography and physiology. Western North American Naturalist 61: 463-472.

Chapter 4. Translating Response into Vulnerability and Management Recommendations

Chapter 4 Talking Points

(1) **Vulnerability is implicated from a variety of measures that have different assumptions.**
(2) **The vulnerability measure(s) used will determine applicability to specific management problems.**
(3) **All assessments contain uncertainty but that need not limit their ability to inform management.**

Vulnerability or the susceptibility of a resource to negative impact is the key measure of a vulnerability assessment. It helps us to interpret climate change response for management purposes. In some cases, vulnerability may be equivalent to prediction of response or observed effects, but in others, further measurement and assumptions will be needed to translate expected response into vulnerability. Because management goals and negative impacts are shaped by human perceptions, climate change response needs to be translated into a measure relevant to contemporary society; this is often achieved by examining response in relationship to something else (e.g., historic baseline, response of other targets, or threshold of suitability). For example, consider models of future tree distribution (Iverson and others 2004, 2008). Vulnerability is not the distribution of a given species at a given time, but how different that projected distribution is from the distribution where the species is currently managed. The distance or amount of overlap between distributions provides a measure of the degree of negative impact or vulnerability and can be used to compare multiple tree species to give a sense of relative vulnerability. A wide variety of measures, both direct and inferred, have been used to estimate vulnerability of a given target to climate change. Assessments can use a single measure of vulnerability, combine several measures, or record identified vulnerabilities in a synthesis. Targets, scope, and scale will affect how vulnerability is quantified (Chapter 2).

4.1 Measures of Vulnerability

The measure of vulnerability is important to understanding assessment conclusions and possible limitations to applying the results. Six common measures of vulnerability to climate change used in natural resource management are outlined below (Box 4.1).

4.1.1 Degree of Recent Change From Historic

Because global and regional climates have been warming for several decades, vulnerability can be measured from recent departure of targets to known background variability (Fig. 4.1). Background or historic levels can be taken from

Box 4.1. Summary of vulnerability measures, common applications, and considerations for use.

Vulnerability measure	Considerations
Observed degree of recent change	No models needed
	Depends on sensitivity of target
	Assumes continuation of observed trends
Modeled departure from baseline	Greater response = greater vulnerability
	Current distributions may not fully represent sensitivity and adaptive capacity
	Inclusion of all key variables
Observations from experiments or past events	Studied conditions correspond to future conditions
	Experiments can only manipulate a few variables
	Limited data available for the past
Proximity to thresholds	Thresholds are difficult to set
Estimated adaptive capacity	Needs to be integrated with exposure and sensitivity
	Unknown relationships between adaptive capacity and response
Relative importance of modeled factors	Accuracy of relationships among model variables
	Inclusion of all key variables

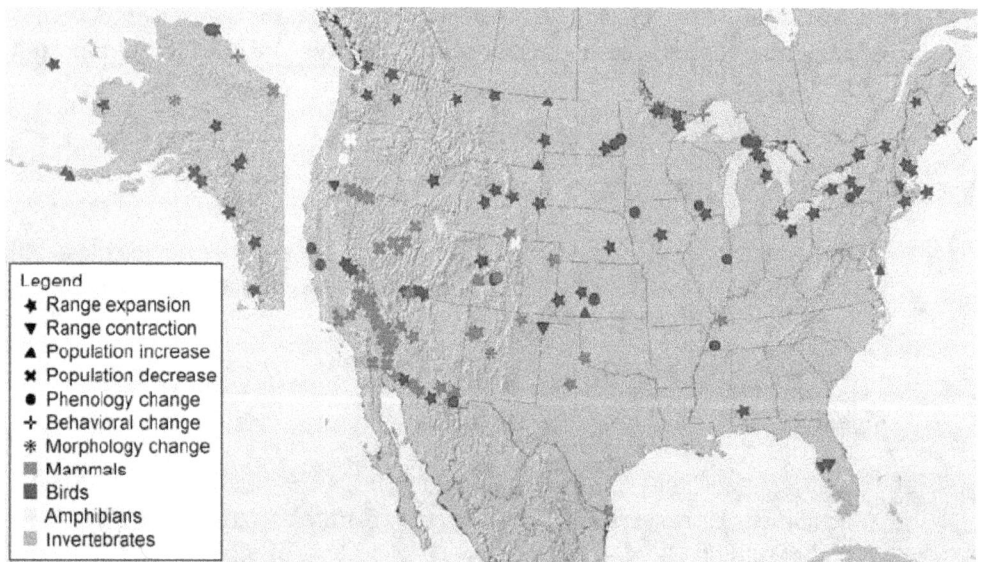

Figure 4.1. Observed response of terrestrial wildlife to climate change effects from 189 studies reviewed by Joyce and others (2008). These patterns can be translated into information that identifies which species might be most affected by future climate conditions. Adapted from Joyce and others (2008).

Legend
- ✦ Range expansion
- ▼ Range contraction
- ▲ Population increase
- ✖ Population decrease
- ● Phenology change
- ✛ Behavioral change
- ✳ Morphology change
- ▮ Mammals
- ▮ Birds
- Amphibians
- ▮ Invertebrates

USDA Forest Service RMRS-GTR-309. 2013.

various sources and time periods as a baseline for comparison. This method is commonly used to assess vulnerability of individual species to climate change but has also been applied to communities. For example, phenological or timing responses to climate change are often based on recent observations, such as the difference in date over the past decade for initial spring bud burst or the arrival date of a migratory bird species. A study of recent shifts in bird migration timing in the fall found differences in the degree of timing change (i.e., vulnerability) by species, depending on migration distance and variability in annual brood number (Jenni and Kery 2003). Spatial measures can also be accommodated, such as the change in distance from the historic center of a species range to the current center. This is akin to methods that use historic conditions (such as the natural range of variability, see case study in Chapter 2) as a benchmark or reference to examine the degree of change in a system. The assumption of this group of approaches is that greater change is indicative of greater vulnerability.

Recent change is an appropriate measure for targets that are particularly sensitive to climate variables allowing for a measurable effect, less so for targets that are resistant at current levels of change. Because the degree of change is measured directly, interactions and multiple contributing factors to response are included, but this also makes it difficult to pinpoint the primary causes for the observed changes. This approach does not require projecting into the future but assumes that the degree of vulnerability in the future, and similarly the rate of climate change, will follow the observed trend, which is uncertain considering that climate effects and interactions are unlikely to be linear.

4.1.2 Degree of Modeled Future Change From a Baseline

The magnitude of departure of future projections of climate, species distributions, biodiversity, and other measures from baseline observations is a common measure of vulnerability (Figs. 4.2, 4.3). Modeling approaches are commonly used for the future projections so targets are limited to those that can be modeled or that can be correlated with modeled variables. Greater divergence between the baseline and the projected future conditions is equated with greater exposure and increasing vulnerability. This measure of vulnerability is useful for large-scale targets such as ecosystems or regions. For smaller scales, a correlative approach is often taken. Distribution models, a common approach, correlate species presence with climate and environmental variables, which can then be used to project distributions give future climate conditions. Vulnerability is the change in distance or overlap of current climate conditions to the projected location of similar conditions. Alternatively, vulnerability might relate to the estimated magnitude or velocity of change. Distribution approaches primarily focus on the exposure aspect of vulnerability, but some efforts include other aspects of vulnerability such as the potential for dispersal. For example, Iverson and others (2004) predicted potential habitat for five tree species in eastern North America by combining a species distribution model with a spatial model of migration potential to estimate the probability of the species colonizing new potential habitat; species with lower colonization potential would be more vulnerable to climate change.

Accuracy of these measures of vulnerability depends on the ability of the model to project future conditions, and considerable discussion has evolved about the limitations of these models and subsequent improvements (see Chapter 3.2). Modeling approaches are numerous, but they can be generally categorized as modeling the future based on observation of outcomes (empirical or statistical models) or based on the processes that determine outcomes (mechanistic or process-based

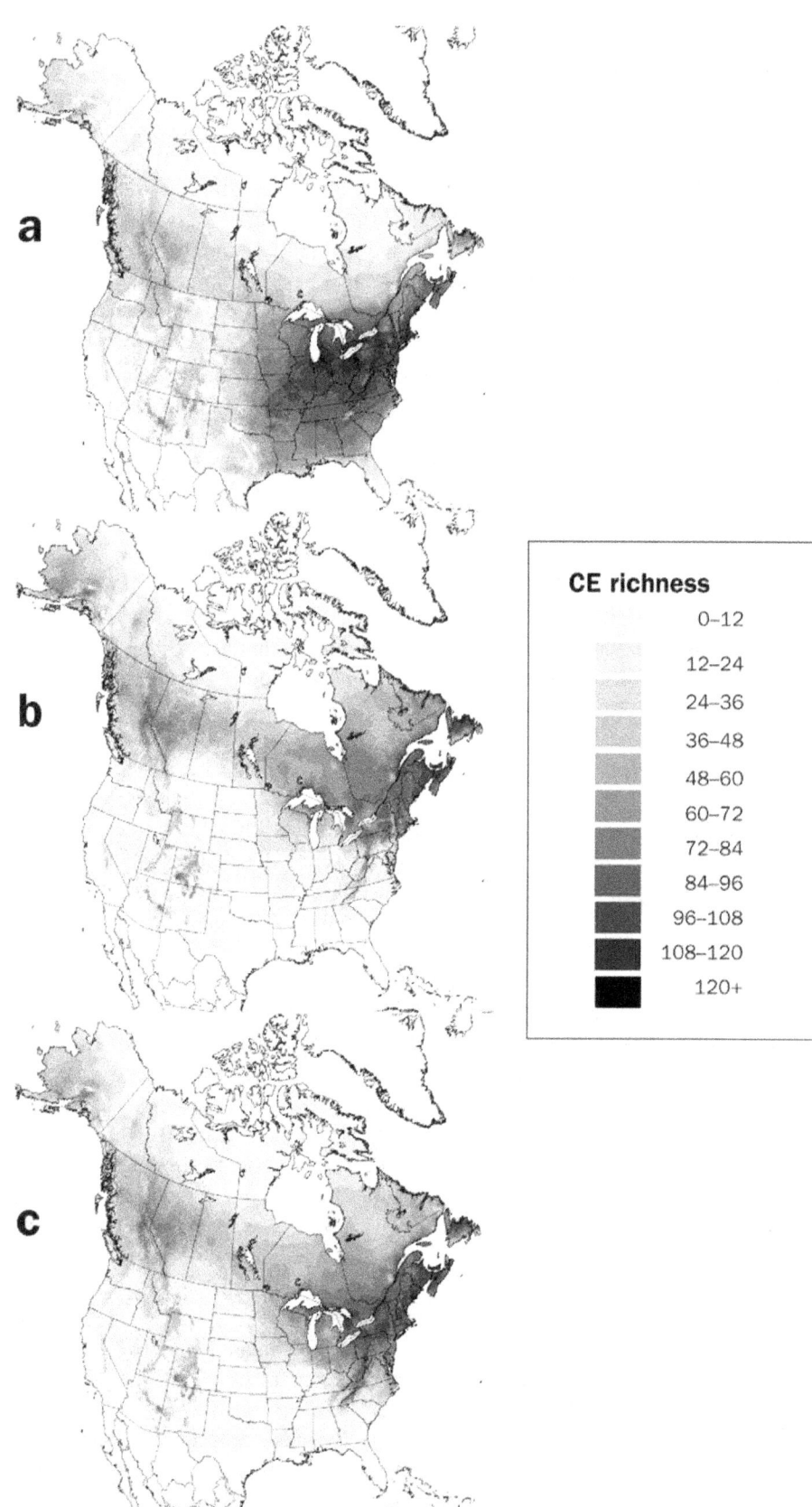

CE richness

0–12

12–24

24–36

36–48

48–60

60–72

72–84

84–96

96–108

108–120

120+

Figure 4.2. Richness of American tree species under current (A) and future (B and C) climate scenarios. Future (B) represents projections under increasing CO_2 whereas future (C) represents conditions with future decrease in CO_2. This study presents an estimate of future effects based upon current understood relationships between tree richness and climate variables. CE=Climate envelope richness. Adapted from McKenney and others 2007.

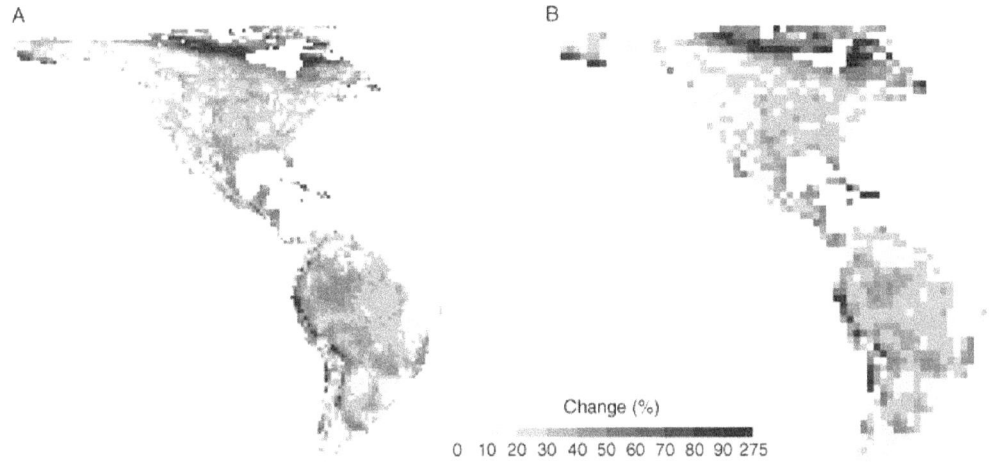

Figure 4.3. An example of how the degree of response (species richness) might be used to measure vulnerability. Here, darker colors represent areas that are expected to experience the greatest change and are therefore at greatest risk of negative impact, in species composition under a mid A1B greenhouse gas scenario. (A) represents projections for a 100 x 100-km grid and (B) represents 200 x 200-km grid projections. Adapted from Lawler and others (2009).

models). Correlative approaches assume that the modeled climate and environmental variables rather than sensitivity or adaptive capacity are the key drivers of distribution and that current distributions can capture ecological limitations of the target (Schmitz and others 2003).

4.1.3 Observed Impacts Under Comparable Conditions

Comparable climate conditions to those projected for the future can be found from the paleoclimate when carbon dioxide levels were much higher, from recent extreme events, or from experimental treatments. Response of the chosen target can be measured or estimated under those comparable conditions to predict climate change response (Figs. 4.4, 4.5). Episodic events, such as drought or El Niño, are expected to be more frequent under a warming climate and are good for identifying the vulnerability of targets because these events occur frequently enough to observe (Fig 4.5). Vulnerability is identified by comparing the target's responses to the episodic event to responses during a period outside the event or from a control site for an experiment. An examination of recent vegetation die-off in the Southwest due to drought and bark beetle infestation highlighted how extreme events and biotic interactions can lead to rapid and large-scale change in the distribution of pinyon (*Pinus edulis*) (Breshears and others 2005). Similarly, paleoclimatic conditions similar to those projected can offer insights into expected responses. Experiments can directly measure the response of a target to climate change by manipulating variables such as CO_2 or temperature and can even be conducted in the field where the target is subject to important ecological processes.

Experiments are often limited to short time periods and only a few climate variables can be manipulated at relatively small scales. Data available from paleoclimatic conditions or extreme events are also limited in terms of spatial distribution, thus limiting the range of targets and responses that can be examined using this approach. While the inclusion of responses to extreme events is relevant given their absence in most models, inference is limited in that responses are generally only examined in the short term and extreme events under future climate

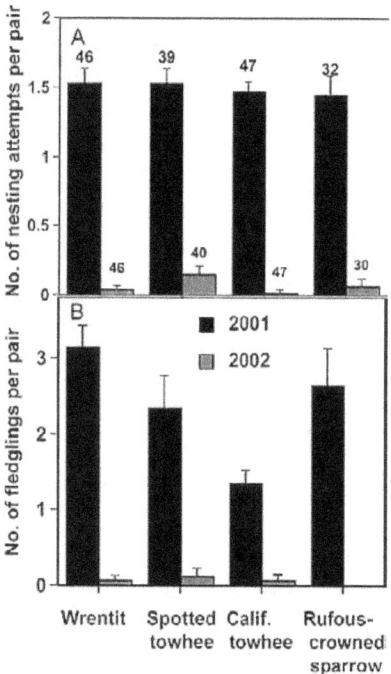

Figure 4.4. Observed changes in nesting attempts and fledglings per pair among four bird species in California due to extreme drought. Year 2002 was the driest year on record for the past 150 years. This study provides an example of how and to what degree future populations might be affected by particular climate trends. Adapted from Bolger and others (2005).

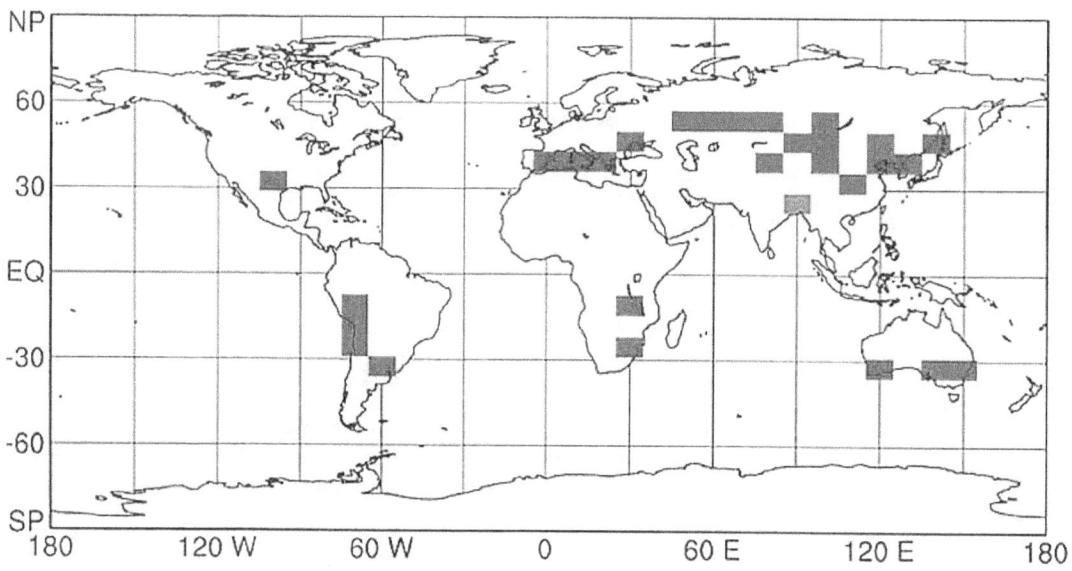

Figure 4.5. Transitions between carbon (C) states: C_4 to C_3 (red) and C_3 to C_4 (blue) grass communities in response to increased temperatures and atmospheric pCO_2 since the last glacial maximum (approximately 20,000 years before present). Adapted from Collatz and others (1998).

change will likely differ from historical events in important ways such as frequency or magnitude. An assessment will also be limited if measures of vulnerability rely on a single climate change stressor, such as drought (Enquist and Gori 2008).

4.1.4 Exceeding Thresholds

Many studies have noted levels or states of target measures at which resilience of individuals or systems is exceeded and a pre-disturbance configuration will not return (CCSP 2009). These are called thresholds or tipping points. Proximity to the identified threshold or to the probability of exceeding a threshold is a measure of vulnerability. Thresholds can be difficult to identify, but this approach recognizes that responses and impacts will not necessarily be linear. In the previous section, we provided a pinyon die-off example of the threshold approach; this study also identified thresholds of water stress that predict tree mortality, which can be used in conjunction with climate projections to assess vulnerability of this species (Breshears and others 2005; Fig. 4.6). The threshold approach also has

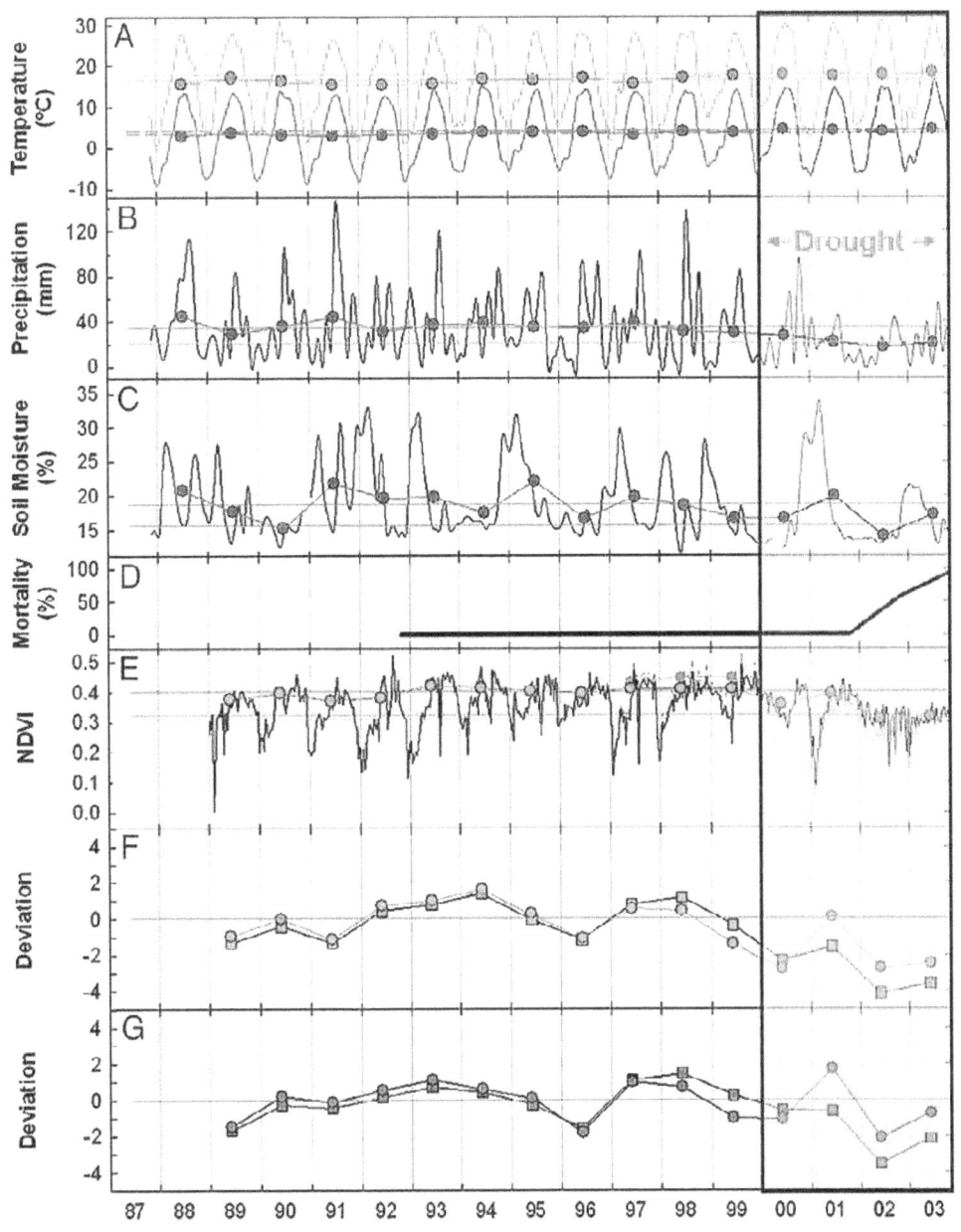

Figure 4.6. Results of this study identified the critical thresholds that lead to widespread mortality in pine species in the Southwest. From Breshears and others (2005). Copyright 2005 National Academy of Sciences, USA.

implications for management in that actions are targeted to a specific level of impact rather than requiring a sustained effort to reduce impacts. Because there is non-linear change in vulnerability over time, the time scale of the assessment and the uncertainty surrounding the threshold level need to be considered carefully.

4.1.5 Capacity to Adapt to Change

Adaptive capacity is a key component of vulnerability, often thought of as a species-specific measure, but it can also apply to individuals or systems as well as to the ability of the managing organization to ameliorate negative impacts (Fig. 4.7). Flexibility, such as behavioral or morphological plasticity, can increase the ability of the target to cope with changing conditions, thus increasing resilience (i.e., reducing vulnerability). Where this plasticity arises from intraspecific genetic variation, it may be heritable and thus provide the basis for adaptation to novel conditions. Examination of population dynamics and variability in the heritable traits that control timing of budburst in the Scottish birch revealed that budburst, although advancing with warmer temperatures, was unlikely to keep up with warming of 2 °C in the next 60 years (Billington and Pellham 1991).

Resilience of ecosystems and communities has been related to level of biodiversity or functional diversity (Naeem 2006; Petchey and Gaston 2009). Dispersal ability, which can confer a species' capacity to track favorable environmental conditions, is an important adaptive strategy that can be measured by mobility, rates of movement, and dispersal vectors. Traits may also characterize adaptive capacity where they are associated with the ability to cope with the expected effects of climate change. For example, species that are habitat or resource generalists may be at an advantage under varying conditions, because they have greater flexibility in habitat use than a species that specializes in a particular habitat or resource (Parmesan 2006). Vulnerability may be measured by the strength of a given capacity measure for alleviating negative impacts, the presence or absence of a distinguishing trait, or as the number of traits possessed that limit the target's

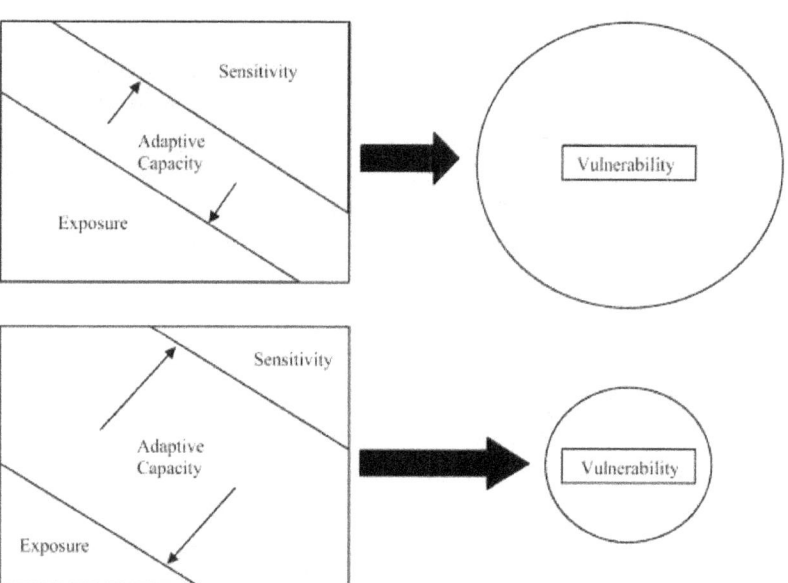

Figure 4.7. Schematic of the relationship between adaptive capacity and species vulnerability. Adaptive capacity affects species vulnerability by modulating exposure and sensitivity. Adapted from Engle 2011.

response to change. Difficulty in addressing vulnerability through traits arises because the strength and nature of the relationship between the adaptive traits and the associated reduction of vulnerability is generally not well known.

4.1.6 Relative Degree of Response to Climate Variation

This measure of vulnerability is commonly conducted using a sensitivity analysis and examines quantitatively how much the target measure changes when model parameters are varied (Fig. 4.8). These analyses start with a modeled representation of climate-related variables (e.g., timing of peak runoff) and the expected response in the target (e.g., aquifer recharge). The relative response or degree of change in the target is determined by varying the climate inputs across a range of values. Sensitivity to the climate variables infers vulnerability. The rangze of climate variables inputted is often the range produced by different emissions scenarios or projections from different global climate models, which is helpful in evaluating the uncertainty surrounding model selection and which climate parameters most affect the target. Keller and others (2005) examined duration of snow cover and its interaction with plants at high altitudes and found duration most sensitive to mean temperature and identified plant habitat zones subject to the greatest advancement in snowmelt, which may indicate greater vulnerability. Sala and others (2000) looked at the relative influence of various drivers on declines in biodiversity by region (Fig. 4.8). Potential management actions can be incorporated into models to evaluate their effectiveness at reducing vulnerability. A model that accurately links the target to climate is critical to this type of analysis.

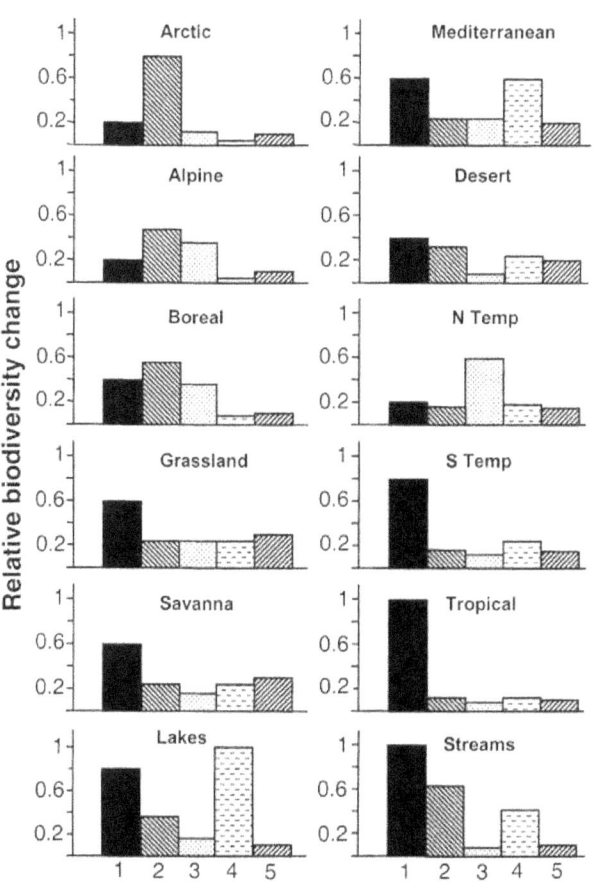

Figure 4.8. Effect of each driver on biodiversity change for each terrestrial biome and freshwater ecosystem type calculated as the product of the expected change of each driver times its impact for each terrestrial biome or freshwater ecosystem. Values are relative to the maximum possible value. Bars: 1, land use; 2, climate; 3, nitrogen deposition; 4, biotic exchange; 5, atmospheric CO_2. From Sala and others (2000). Reprinted with permission from American Association for the Advancement of Science (AAAS).

4.2 Informing Natural Resource Management Recommendations

Vulnerability measures provide a ranking of vulnerability and, in doing so, identify priority targets or actions (Table 4.1). In their review, Peterson and others (2011) outlined how to translate climate vulnerability data into adaptive management options (Fig. 4.9). Implementation of adaptive management strategies combines climate data and prioritization schemes to develop and assess management actions that are most likely to achieve management goals to promote resistance and resilience or facilitate transition. Ranking species according to their relative vulnerability provides a means to identify priority species and potential actions that, implemented in the near future, might prevent further population decline. This may also apply to critical ecosystems services, such as water quality, where assessment targets may include variables (processes, critical species) believed essential to continued functioning. Vulnerability measures may also consider how well current management strategies reflect the likely future state of the system under study. A vulnerability assessment that considers the degree of change in vegetation community distributions identifies vulnerable systems with a high likelihood of not persisting under future climate regimes. This type of assessment might also identify species that are likely to colonize the area in the future and thereby provide information regarding potential new management goals. Sensitivity to climate change as inferred by observations of response to past climate change, is a good measure of which species or habitats are likely to need the greatest degree of intervention. Probability of occurrence or likelihood of distribution shifts are useful measures to gauge the applicability of current management strategies under future conditions. Degree of vulnerability, as generated with a quantified vulnerability score, can inform both short- and long-term goals.

Table 4.1. Summary of common measures of vulnerability, applicable time scales, key limitations, and common applications.

Measure of vulnerability	Time scales	Limitations	Common applications
Degree of recent change from historic	Short-term only (extrapolate to longer)	Sensitive targets only	Phenology of flowering plants and migrating birds
Degree of modeled future change from baseline	Any	Relation of target to modeled climate variables	Species distributions, exposure
Observed impacts under comparable conditions	Any (but older data more limited)	Historic or paleo record data available, manipulations of few variables	Effects of extreme events and high levels of CO_2 at a large scale, experimental response in plants
Exceeding thresholds	Any	Difficulty identifying ecological thresholds	Vegetation communities
Ability to adapt to change	Varies by target	Relationship between adaptations and population parameters	Single species
Relative degree of response to climate variation	Any	Relation of target to modeled climate variables	Single species

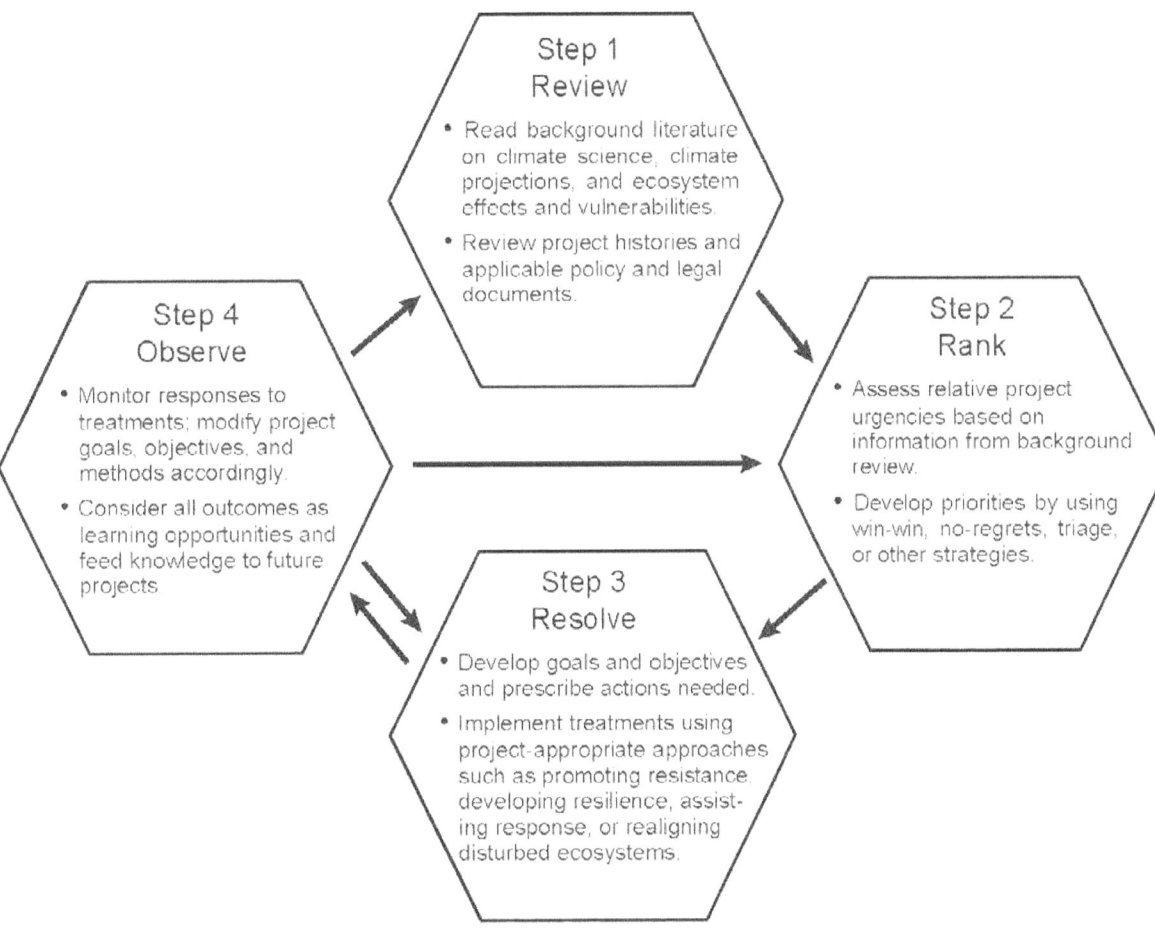

Figure 4.9. Steps for developing and implementing adaptation options. This diagram, first presented in Peterson and others (2011), represents an iterative process and includes repetitive review and ranking steps.

4.2.1 Planning for the Future

Vulnerability assessments can provide valuable information for what and how natural resources may be affected by climate change and, thus, facilitate proactive management (Fig 4.10). Identification of vulnerable resources helps to set management priorities and the underlying causes of vulnerability elucidate intervention points for management. For example, Bagne and Finch (2012) found high vulnerability in Morafkai's desert tortoise in southern Arizona due to timing changes in herbaceous growth, susceptibility of succulents to fire and invasive plants, and temperature-determined sex ratios, which suggest intervention points of fire management, invasive plant control, and enhancement of vegetative cover, particularly in cooler microhabitats. Managers might use a vulnerability assessment focused on habitat characteristics to identify how climate will affect the suitability of future relocation sites or effectiveness of reintroduction activities. Conserving biologically important landscapes and species are a critical component of maintaining biodiversity, especially in the face of climate change. At the same time, managers and researchers recognize that successful strategies are increasingly focused on maintaining habitat and ecosystem function over individual elements. Vulnerability assessments focused on climate impacts to biodiversity can provide information

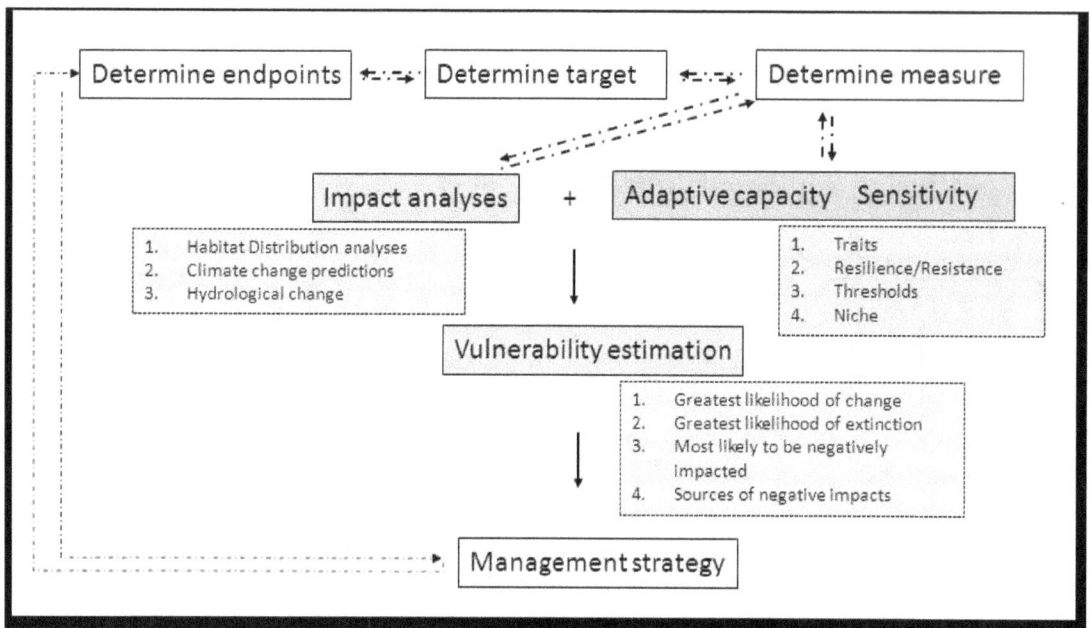

Figure 4.10. Example of work-flow used to create a vulnerability assessment that is translated to on-the-ground management strategies. Endpoints are determined by the questions and objectives of managers and are largely influenced by management strategies to mitigate, improve, or facilitate response to climate change. Target selection depends upon the desired endpoint and influences the relevant measures used to gauge target vulnerability. Targets also influence the availability of relevant measures.

on potential hotspots and refugia (e.g., Davison and others 2012), thus allowing managers to focus resources where there is the greatest benefit. Vulnerability assessments are also useful for identifying monitoring strategies, especially where current programs exclude potentially sensitive species.

4.2.2 Promoting Resistance and Resilience

Vulnerability assessments can be used to gauge the effectiveness of management strategies focused along a wide biological spectrum as well as determine the best practices for increasing resilience and resistance of our landscapes under climate change (Peterson and others 2011; Lou Comer and others 2012). Species-level assessments are valuable for identifying high priority species and potential new sources of concern. For instance, a manager might use a vulnerability assessment to determine whether ecologically important species might be negatively impacted by climate impacts or whether an invasive species will be favored by future conditions. Depending on the degree and nature of the change, managers can choose whether specific areas or species warrant actions to mitigate loss of biodiversity or prevent establishment of exotic species. For species already of concern, vulnerability assessments can improve our ability to foresee and reduce additive stressor impacts that arise from both the direct and indirect consequences of climate change. Restoration practices to enhance resilience include habitat restoration and reestablishment of natural and important disturbance processes such as floods and fire. A vulnerability assessment that compares the degree of expected change across the landscape could be used to prioritize restoration activities to areas with the greatest promise for sustaining populations. Alternatively, post-fire seeding activities may be informed by estimations of future conditions produced by a vulnerability assessment. Assessments are also helpful for facilitated transformation strategies

(USFS Scorecard Guidelines), which aim to work with anticipated changes in order to facilitate transitions to new stable states with minimal ecological disruption. Adaptation strategies aimed at improving genetic adaptive capacity, translocation and relocation activities can be informed by multiple types of vulnerability measures and assessments.

4.2.3 Landscape-Level Planning

Future climate envelopes inform landscape practices that involve the development and preservation of corridors, relocation of individuals, and preservation of high quality habitats (Glick and others 2011). Increasingly, conservation and management must cross political and jurisdictional boundaries. Common objectives and strategies for maintaining wildlife and habitat across landscapes can be informed by a vulnerability assessment conducted at regional levels or involving species relevant to multiple stakeholder groups. For example, increasing adaptive capacity of populations threatened by climate change commonly involves improving genetic stock through translocations. Assessments that outline future suitable conditions can guide practices that aim to improve the expression of drought tolerance or other favorable traits through translocations, which often must cross political boundaries.

4.2.4 Limitations

Predicting response to climate change and measuring climate change vulnerability is difficult because it is part of a complex and dynamic process. Vulnerability measures address effects through various means that highlight unique aspects of natural systems. The relevance of any one measure of change or impact relates to its capacity to accurately provide information regarding future trends and the potential for actions to ameliorate or mitigate effects. The dynamic and progressive nature of climate change also requires managers to carefully consider values and management goals. Divergence from current or historic conditions highlights the need for managers to identify appropriate and desirable benchmarks for natural resources. As noted in Chapters 1 and 2, benchmarks are often set on reference conditions but, in light of climate change, are now moving away from emulating historic conditions and toward a focus on preserving ecosystem function and services. Our understanding of the full range of potential changes and responses, as well as our ability to address them, will grow as more researchers and managers participate in the assessment process.

4.2.5 Assessment Tools and Guidance

Vulnerability assessments and the methods used to generate them can supply managers with the tools and resources needed to make decisions that incorporate considerations of climate change and climate change vulnerability (Fig. 4.10). There are a number of tools available to facilitate vulnerability assessment, several of which are specifically designed to inform management decisions (Table 4.2). Many of these sources (e.g., VEMAP) provide estimates of future impact, which can then be used within an assessment of vulnerability. Some sources provide critical baseline data, such as natural history information, that are useful for conducting analyses or applying an index scoring systems (e.g., NatureServe Explorer and BISON-M). Others (e.g., Treeage Pro) are methods to use the results of a vulnerability assessment to create management strategies or guide decision-making processes. These decision support tools are particularly useful for addressing issue relating to the uncertainty inherent in climate and distribution modeling efforts. Several networks and exchanges have developed in response to the increasing need for cross boundary collaboration. TACCIMO (Template for Assessing Climate Change Information and Management Options) was developed to provide an avenue for distributing scientific data to land managers. Similarly, ongoing efforts in the ILAP aim to synthesize and provide products to managers and conservationists base on output from many of the modeling methods discussed in this chapter. Additional tools can be found on the Forest Service Climate Change Resource Centers (SCRC, http://www.fs.fed.us/ccrc/). Another source for climate data, both historic and projected, is the Western Water Assessment page, which contains data for terrestrial and hydrological systems: http://wwa.colorado.edu/climate_change/trendpro.html. In addition, a number of approaches have been developed that allow users to compare adaptive management strategies. These may range from specific analyses of risk (informed by products produced during a vulnerability assessment process) to more general conceptual frameworks, which consider either directly or indirectly the impacts of climate change for management targets and try to identify specific management objectives or options.

Table 4.2. Resources, including data repositories, for exploring management options and for use in climate change vulnerability assessments. Asterisks indicate data resource.

Name	Description	Target/scope	Available from:
Data Sources/Tools			
U.S. Geological Survey's Gap Analysis Program (GAP)*	Online tool to aid in analysis and retrieval of species distribution data.	Land cover and vertebrate species	http://www.nbii.gov/portal/server.pt/community/gap_online_analysis_tool/1851
Bureau of Reclamation's Bias Corrected and Downscaled WCRP CMIP3 Climate and Hydrology Projections*	Temperature, precipitation, evaporation, and streamflow characteristics are available for download from website.	Climate and hydrology of western U.S. watersheds, rivers, and streams	http://gdo-dcp.ucllnl.org/downscaled_cmip_projections/dcpInterface.html
National Atlas*	Provides GIS format data on land cover, land use, hydrography, climate, and digital elevation models.	Varies	http://www.nationalatlas.gov/atlasftp.html
Multi-Resolution Land Characteristics Consortium*	Landcover databases.	Bioregions	http://www.mrlc.gov/mrlc2k_nlcd.asp
Vegetation/Ecosystem modeling and analysis Project- VEMtAP*	Uses historical and future projected climate data, soils and vegetation maps, and a number of process models to project communities across the globe. Produces spatially explicit information regarding terrestrial ecosystem sensitivity to elevated CO_2 and climate change.	Vegetation types/biomes	http://www.cgd.ucar.edu/vemap/ also see Feenstra 2009
ClimateWizard*	Estimate historical and future temperature and precipitation changes as absolute or percent change.	Climate variables	http://www.climatewizard.org/
Biota Information System of New Mexico (BISON-M)	Biological information and summaries.	New Mexico species	http://www.bison-m.org/
IUCN Red List	Uses current threats and population trends and related information to determine risk of future population declines.	Threatened plants and animals globally	http://www.iucnredlist.org/

Table 4.2. *Continued.*

Name	Description	Target/scope	Available from:
Wyoming Natural Diversity Database	Biological information and summaries.	Wyoming	http://www.uwyo.edu/wyndd/
NatureServe Explorer*	Biological information and summaries.	Plants and animals of U.S. and Canada	http://www.natureserve.org/explorer/
U.S. drought monitor (current conditions and projections)*	Historical, current, and future maps of drought levels.	U.S.	http://droughtmonitor.unl.edu/
Climate Change Tree and Bird Atlases*	Current and future projections of species under climate change and considering current management issues.	Eastern U.S.—134 trees, 147 birds	http://www.fs.fed.us/ccrc/tools/atlas.shtml
Climate-FVS [Forest Vegetation Simulator]	Model that relies on modified FVS growth equations to predict performance under climate change.	Tree species	Crookston and others 2010
U.S. National Phenology Network*	Integrates data collection and houses database of literature and observations regarding species phenology.	Plants and animals of U.S. and Canada	http://www.usanpn.org/home

Network and Exchanges

Name	Description	Target/scope	Available from:
Southwest Climate Change Network	Regional assessment of climate change impacts on habitat and watershed. Includes workshops for managers and planners to introduce adaptation options.	Southwest U.S.	http://www.southwestclimatechange.org/
Integrated Landscape Assessment Project (ILAP)*	Collaborative effort to explore dynamics of land ownership, habitat disturbance, and climate change. Provides data, tools, and information.	Currently in development for SW and Oregon	http://oregonstate.edu/inr/ilap
Template for Assessing Climate Change Impacts and Management Options (TACCIMO)*	Center provides forest landowners, managers, and scientists with the latest research and expertise concerning environmental threats to forests.	Forests	http://www.sgcp.ncsu.edu:8090/
Landfire	Geospatial data regarding land classifications across the U.S. as it relates to climate and disturbance. Typically reports departure from reference conditions.	Ecosystems, habitat, and vegetation characteristics	http://www.landfire.gov/

Statistical Decision Support Statistical methods to estimate potential response of targets to risk factors and uncertainty. Bernliner and others 2000; Prato 2009

Name	Description	Target/scope	Available from:
Bayesian Analysis Toolkit	Software package that allows users to compare model predictions to data, test model validity, and extract values of free parameters of models.	Uncertainty measure	http://www.mppmu.mpg.de/bat/
Treeage Pro	Decision support software that uses various methods to distinguish between models and decisions options.	Decision support	www.treeage.com/products.index.html
Delphi Decision Aid site	Data gathering tool for forecasting purposes.	Forecasts of climate change	armstrong.wharton.upenn.edu/delphi2/
BIOMOD	Ecological niche factor analysis. BIOMOD is a computer platform for ensemble forecasting of species distributions, enabling the treatment of a range of methodological uncertainties in models and the examination of species-environment relationships.	Environmental envelopes	http://r-forge.r-project.org/projects/biomod/

Literature Cited

Bagne, Karen E., Deborah M. Finch. 2012. Vulnerability of species to climate change in the Southwest: threatened, endangered, and at-risk species at the Barry M. Goldwater Range, Arizona. Gen. Tech. Rep. RMRS-GTR-284. Fort Collins, CO: U.S. Department of Agriculture, Forest Service, Rocky Mountain Research Station. 139 p.

Billington, H.L., and J. Pelham. 1991. Genetic Variation in the Date of Budburst in Scottish Birch Populations: Implications for Climate Change. Functional Ecology 5: 403-409.

Bolger, D.T., M.A. Patten, and D.C. Bostock. 2005. Avian reproductive failure in response to an extreme climatic event. Oecologia 142: 398-406.

Breshears, D.D., N.S. Cobb, P.M. Rich, [and others]. 2005. Regional vegetation die-off in response to global-change-type drought. Proceedings of the National Academy of Sciences 102:15144-15148.

Fagre, D.B., C.W. Charles, C.D. Allen, C. Birkeland, F.S. Chapin III, P.M. Groffman, G.R Guntenspergen, A.K. Knapp, A.D. McGuire, P.J. Mulholland, D.P.C. Peters, D.D. Roby, and G. Sugihara. 2009. Thresholds of climate change in Ecosystems: Final Report, Synthesis and Assessment Product 4.2. : U.S. Geological Survey A report by the U.S. Climate Change Science Program and the Subcommittee on Global Change Research. 157+ p. Collatz, G.J., J.A. Berry, and J.S. Clark. 1998. Effects of climate and atmospheric CO_2 partial pressure on the global distribution of C4 grasses: present, past, and future. Oecologia 114: 441-454.

Davison, J.E, S. Coe, D. Finch, [and others]. 2012. Bringing indices of species vulnerability to climate change into geographic space: an assessment across the Coronado National Forest. Biodiversity Conservation 21: 189-204.

Enquist, C., and D. Gori. 2008a. Implications of Recent Climate Change and Conservation Priorities in New Mexico. The Nature Conservancy New Mexico Conservation Science Program, 79 p. Available at: http://www.nmconservation.org. (Accessed December 2008.)

Iverson, L.R., A.M. Prasad, S.N. Matthews, and M. Peters. 2008. Estimating potential habitat for 134 eastern US tree species under six climate scenarios. Forest Ecology and Management 254(3): 390-406.

Iverson, L.R., M.W. Schwartz, and A.M. Prasad. 2004. Potential colonization of newly available tree-species habitat under climate change: an analysis for five eastern US species. Landscape Ecology 19: 787-799.

Jenni, L., and M. Kery. 2003. Timing of autumn bird migration under climate change: advances in long–distance migrants, delays in short-distance migrants. Proceedings of the Royal Society, London 270: 1467-1471.

Joyce, L.A., C.H. Flather, and M. Koopman. 2008. WHPRP Final Project Report: 1.B: Analysis of Potential Impacts of Climate Change on Wildlife Habitats in the U.S. Available at: http://www.tribesandclimatechange.org/docs/tribes_214.pdf.

Keller, F., S. Goyette, and M. Beniston. 2005. Sensitivity analysis of snow cover to climate change scenarios and their impact on plant habitats in alpine terrain. Climatic Change 72:299-319.

Lawler, J.J., S.L. Shafer, D. White, [and others]. 2009. Projected climate-induced faunal change in the Western Hemisphere. Ecology 90: 588-597.

Parmesan, C. 2006. Ecological and Evolutionary Responses to Recent Climate Change. Annual Review of Ecology, Evolution, and Systematics 37: 637-669.

Petchey, Owen L., and Kevin J. Gaston. 2009. Effects on ecosystem resilience of biodiversity, extinctions, and the structure of regional species pools. Theoretical Ecology 2:177-187.

Peterson, D.L., C.I. Millar, L.A. Joyce, M.J. Furniss, J.E. Halofsky, R.P. Neilson, and T. Lyn Morelli. 2011. Responding to climate change in National Forests: a guidebook for developing adaptation options. Gen. Tech. Rep. PNW-GTR-855. Portland, OR: U.S. Department of Agriculture, Forest Service, Pacific Northwest Research Station. 109 p.

Schmitz, O.J., E. Post, C.E. Burns, and K.M. Johnston. 2003. Ecosystem Responses to Global Climate Change: Moving Beyond Color Mapping. BioScience 53(12):1199-1205.

USDA Forest Service. 2011. Navigating the Climate Change Performance Scorecard. A Guide for National Forest and Grasslands, Version 2. Available at: http://www.fs.fed.us/climatechange/advisor/scorecard/scorecard-guidance-08-2011.pdf.

Chapter 5. Vulnerability of Southwestern Species and Ecosystems to Climate Change: A Review

5.1 Introduction

Climate change vulnerability assessments link scientific information of future change to specific features, species, or areas that must be managed to successfully mitigate the negative consequences of climate change for natural ecosystems. Ideally, vulnerability assessments would provide a comprehensive view of both small and large issues regarding species conservation across multiple regions of interest. In reality, the body of literature available for managers for any one region is immense and can be difficult to access, and few publications fulfill the specific characteristics of a climate change vulnerability assessments (see Chapter 1) that make them useful to managers. These shortcomings limit our capacity to understand and interpret the ecologically relevant issues relating to climate changes. In this chapter, we review and synthesize the current body of climate change vulnerability assessment literature for southwestern species, habitats, and ecosystems to provide a starting point upon which to build comprehensive and targeted assessments and plans in the future.

The Southwest United States (henceforth, "SW") has undergone rapid expansion in the last half of the century with consequences for resident populations and the natural environment. Climate projections for the United States indicate that the SW will experience more extreme change with respect to temperature increases and drought than other regions (Fig. 5.1). These changes exacerbate existing problems with sustaining valued natural resources. For example, longer droughts and higher temperatures will reduce the already scarce water sources critical to plants, fish, and wildlife as well as the large human population that occupies the region. It is imperative to address these issues and develop a clear understanding of where and to what degree climate change will affect SW species and habitats in order that future management and development plans can be created to effectively balance human and environmental needs.

As discussed in Chapters 3 and 4, vulnerability assessments include a wide variety of approaches and measures. This is reflected in the information available for SW systems, which encompass a broad array of methods and output. Within this review, we identify trends where studies overlap and gaps in our knowledge, and we discuss implications for future assessment work, climate change studies and management plans. We focus primarily on synthesizing climate change vulnerability assessments that relate specifically to natural resource management than on the large and developing body of literature that addresses human-environmental systems (see Turner and others 2003 for discussion). We identify 12 reviews that summarize our understanding of climate projections and potential effects for the SW (Table 5.1). We have also compiled articles that contain information either used in SW assessments or of value for conducting future assessments of the SW (Appendix 2).

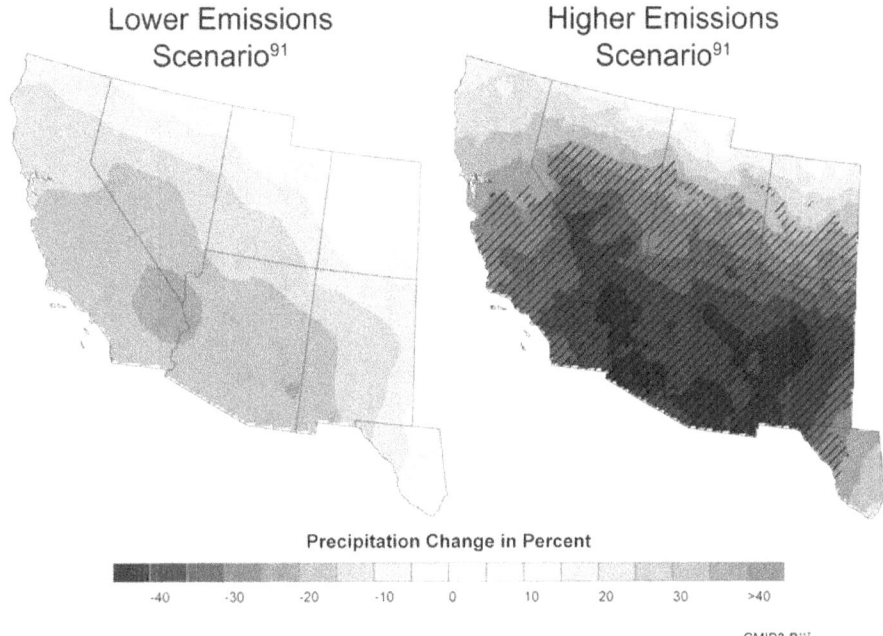

Lower Emissions
Scenario[91]

Higher Emissions
Scenario[91]

Precipitation Change in Percent

-40   -30   -20   -10   0   10   20   30   >40

CMIP3-B[117]

Figure 5.1. Figure from the U.S. Global Change Research Program's 2009 report showing relative changes in precipitation. Predicted change in spring precipitation for 2080-2099 as compared to 1961-1979 for lower and higher emission scenarios. Hatched areas indicate greatest confidence. Report available at: http://nca2009.globalchange.gov/southwest

Percentage change in March-April-May precipitation for 2080-2099 compared to 1961-1979 for a lower emissions scenario[91] (left) and a higher emissions scenario91 (right). Confidence in the projected changes is highest in the hatched areas.

5.2 Methods

For this review, we compiled assessments that provided new information regarding species or habitat vulnerability to climate change in the SW. We focused on assessments with a strong biogeographic content, using Google Scholar and the Template for Assessing Climate Change Information and Management Options (TACCIMO) website (http://www.sgcp.ncsu.edu:8090/) and other online resources for climate change research and management (see Table 4.2). We concentrated on documents that fulfill our working definition of a climate change vulnerability assessment: they examine one or more aspects of vulnerability to identify species, habitats, or biomes that are most likely to suffer negative consequences in response to warming trends. We distinguished between products that synthesize current information (Table 5.1) and those that attempt to identify or assess vulnerability (Table 5.2). Vulnerability assessments are specific in nature (see Chapters 1, 4), but the question of future vulnerability in the SW and a comprehensive discussion of such at times requires a broader discussion of studies that address particular aspects of the vulnerability question. Therefore, we include publications that deal with important aspects of species or habitat vulnerability to climate change though they do not constitute a formal vulnerability assessment per se (e.g., Bradley 2009; Notaro and others 2012; Peery and others 2012; Lawler and others 2009). In addition, we have compiled a list of 47 studies presented in Appendix 2 that address several important aspects of climate change vulnerability but are not included in the following discussion.

Table 5.1. Reviews and syntheses of climate change projections and impacts for species and habitat specific to the SW United States.

Source	Description	Target	Topic	Location	Habitat type
Chambers and Pellant 2008	Reviews projections and implications of climate change for water quantity and quality for wild and domestic species. Identify a number of trends in response to changes in temperature and CO_2.	Plants/ habitat	Climate change	Great Basin, Columbia Plateau, Colorado Plateau	Rangelands
Dale and others 2001	Reviews climate change effects on disturbance processes, including fire, insect, and pathogen outbreak; introduced species and drought; hurricanes; ice storms; windstorms; landslides; and interactions of various disturbances. Discusses strategies for dealing with forest disturbance. Includes socioeconomic considerations.	Disturbance and climate change	Climate and disturbance	U.S.	Forests and Grasslands
Garin and Lenart 2007	Reviews the trends and latest research. Concluded that temperature effects trump uncertainty associated with precipitation because water is very likely to become less available due to temperature effects.	Water availability	Climate change	SW U.S.	Water resources
Hughes and Diaz 2008	Compiles data and information on future climate impacts for arid lands with particular focus on the effect of increased variability on the provision of ecosystem services.	Climate	Climate change	Interior Western U.S.	Arid lands
Kolivras and Comrie 2004	Reviews potential consequences and observed changes to infectious diseases in the SW U.S.	Animals	Disease	SW U.S.	Various
Lenart and others 2007	Reviews the major expected climate changes for the SW. Elaborates on some of the indirect, downstream causes (e.g., monsoon seasons, soil moisture) and discusses recent findings.	Water, forests, grassland	Climate projections	SW U.S.	Forests and grasslands
Lynn and others 2011	Reviews direct and indirect aspects of social vulnerability to climate change.	Socio-economic	Social vulnerability	U.S.	Economic sectors
McPherson and Weltzin 2000	Summarizes literature regarding past vegetation change and importance of various disturbances. Identifies experiments necessary to determine causal mechanisms underlying current and future change. Also evaluates the effects and importance of disturbance and climate change on plant communities.	Livestock, native vertebrates and invertebrates	Disturbance and climate change	Southeastern Arizona and southwestern New Mexico	Rangelands
Perry and others 2012	Reviews direct and indirect impacts of climate change and discusses research priorities and strategies (preserving reservoirs as a strategy).	Water	Global change	Western North America	Water systems
Pettit and Naiman 2007	Reviews fire effects for soil and vegetation and discusses adaptation of systems to fire and future implications under climate change.	Water	Fire	Western Oregon	Arid savanna
Poff and others 2011	Reviews literature to date regarding threats to riparian systems. Climate change is one of many considerations.	Water	Threats	Western North America	Riparian habitats
Sammis 2001	Discusses current, past, and future climate of New Mexico.	Climate	Climate	New Mexico	Various
Vasquez-Leon and others 2003	A comparative assessment of climate vulnerability: agriculture and ranching on both sides of the U.S.-Mexico border.	Social and economic sectors	Socio-economic	SW U.S.	Various

Table 5.2. Climate change vulnerability assessments that contain information for the SW United States. We indicate the scale and spatial focus of the assessment as well as identify the emphasis and primary methods for determining or measuring vulnerability. Climate parameters are listed as reported. "na" indicates not applicable or not available.

Source	Scale	Location	Emphasis	Method	Tools/Measures	Time frame or conditions
Archer and Predick 2008	Regional	SW U.S.	Plant species and habitats; special focus on invasive	Identifies species and habitats that will undergo greatest change	Reviews issues and identifies impacts of expected climate change using logical progression of known consequences for the commonly agreed upon increases in temperature and changes to hydrological regimes.	na
Bagne and Finch 2012	State/local	Southern Arizona	Animal species	Quantifies species traits/vulnerability index	System for Assessing Vulnerability of Species (SAVS) to Climate Change	30- to 50-year future window
Bagne and Finch 2013	State/local	Southern Arizona	Animal species	Quantifies species traits/vulnerability index	System for Assessing Vulnerability of Species (SAVS) to Climate Change	30- to 50-year future window
Bradley 2009	National	U.S.	Bromus trectorum	Identifies likelihood of presence: areas of greatest impact	Developed a bioclimatic envelope model for cheatgrass across the western U.S. Compared using Mahalanobis distance and Maxent to define climate suitability. Future climate from 10 AOGCMS under the A1B emission scenario.	2090-2100
Buckley 2008	National	North America	Animal species	Compares energetic costs among populations	Bioenergetic model	Doubling of CO_2
Christensen and Lettenmaier 2006	Local	Colorado River Basin	Hydrological systems (flow dynamics)	Identifies degree of expected change	Used macroscale hydrology and water resource models and climate data from 11 GCMs under 2 emission scenarios.	2010-2039, 2040-2069, and 2070-2099
Coe and others 2012	State/local	Sky Islands, Arizona	Animal species	Quantifies species traits/vulnerability index	System for Assessing Vulnerability of Species (SAVS) to Climate Change	30- to 50-year future window
Comer and others 2012	Regional/local	Sonoran and Mojave deserts, U.S.	Focal natural communities (plants)	Identifies habitats with greatest vulnerability	Uses a climate change vulnerability index combined with estimates of future climate (ensemble model of six GCMs) and disturbance change as well as impacts to keystone species to generate vulnerability scores.	2060
Currie 2001	National	U.S.	Animal and plant species richness	Identifies changes in biodiversity	Used multiple regression to relate richness to climate variables derived from climate atlases, published maps of geographic ranges, and CCC GCM models.	Doubling of CO_2
Enquist and Gori 2008	State	New Mexico	Comprehensive	Identify areas of greatest vulnerability	Climate Wizard, measure of moisture stress, drought sensitive species and habitats	2030, 2060
Enquist and others 2008	State	New Mexico	Hydrological	Identify areas of greatest vulnerability	Climate Wizard, measure of moisture stress, biodiversity	2030, 2060
Foden and others 2008	Global	Global	Animal species	Quantifies species traits	IUCN Vulnerability Index	Ongoing

Table 5.2. Continued.

Source	Scale	Location	Emphasis	Method	Tools/Measures	Time frame or conditions
Friggens and others 2013	State/local	New Mexico	Animal species	Quantifies species traits/vulnerability index	System for Assessing Vulnerability of Species (SAVS) to Climate Change	30- to 50-year future window
Gonzales and others 2010	Global	Global	Ecotones	Quantifies species traits and identifies elements at greatest risk of impact	Vulnerability classification framework using IPCC uncertainty and a probabilistic framework. MC1 vegetation model; nine GCM-emission scenario combinations (IPCC).	2100
Hansen and others 2001	National	U.S.	Plant (tree) species and communities and animal richness	Identifies greatest threats/species that will undergo greatest change	Synthesize of current knowledge and four biodiversity models: MAPSS, DISTRIB, Response surface model and Currie models. Four equilibrium and three transient GCMs under six scenarios.	2100/doubling of CO_2
Hauer and others 1997	Regional	Rocky Mountains	Hydrological systems (elements)	Identifies elements at greatest risk of impact	Reviews of past and current conditions and hypothesizes about future climate conditions and its relationship to hydrological (and biological) processes. Discusses biogeochemistry, fluvial stuff, and biota of river and lake ecosystems.	na
Hurd and Coonrod 2008	Regional	SW U.S.	Hydrological systems	Identifies systems (ecological and economic) at greatest risk of impact	Hydro-economic models, WATBAL, hydroelectric model the General Algebraic Model System (GAMS) under nine scenarios (three baseline only considered socio factors). Estimates of output streamflow and runoff, reservoir evaporation rate, agricultural use, and urban water demand. HADCM3, CSIRO, NOAA, GFDL0 used to generate six scenarios.	2000, 2030, and 2080
Joyce and Birdsey 2001	National	U.S.	Plant communities (forests)	Synthesizes/conducts comparative analysis of studies measuring change	Biogeochemical models: MAPSS, DOLY, BIOME2, BIOME3 and climate data available via 2nd and 4th Assessment Report (multiple scenario combinations).	
Joyce and others 2008	National	U.S.	Animal communities, habitat change	Estimated/ranked species by degree change	Review of documented climate related changes to estimate degree of habitat overlap, habitat area shift, and climate shift degree of expected climate change. Based upon three GCM, two emission scenarios, and two ecological assumptions regarding plant sensitivity to elevated CO_2.	2100
Julius and others 2006 (Stromberg and others 2006)	Regional	SW U.S.	Hydrological systems (rivers)	Identifies current status and potential for vulnerability	Descriptive with classification based on current features.	na
Kupfer and others 2005	State/local	Sky Island ecosystem	Ecotones	Identify areas of greatest change/impact	Linked plant maps, topographic data, and estimated climate variables (mean daily temp high and low, precipitation for 60-m pixels using MT-CLIM [mountain microclimate simulator]) to create predictive vegetation model. Used manually derived climate scenarios: range of mean low temperature (+1 +5) and precipitation (-10% +100) regimes.	mean temperatures: 1, 2, 3, 4, and 5 °C and precipitation:10, 25, 50, and 100%

Citation	Scale	Subject	Purpose	Description	Time period
Lawler and others 2009	West Hemisphere	Animals	Identify areas of greatest change/impact	Used BCE (random tree) to generate data on future distributions and calculates an index based on the number of "new" or "missing" species per grid cell on maps as well as a "turnover" value representing both species gain and losses.	2071-2100
Lawler and others 2010	West Hemisphere	Amphibians	Identify areas and species of greatest change/impact	Three-prong approach that used BCE (Random Forest), mapped representations of species range limits, and maps depicting areas most likely to experience decreased moisture to identify areas of greatest turnover (greatest geographical vulnerability). Climate conditions based on 20 climate simulations under B1 and A2 scenarios.	2071-2100
McKenney and others 2007	Continent — North America	Plant species (trees)	Identifies species that will undergo greatest change	ANUCLIM software with presence data. Model baseline data were taken from 30-year climate station averages (1971-2000). Climate projections were generated from Canadian GCM, UK-based Hadley GCM and Australian-based Commonwealth Scientific and Industrial Research Organization GCM under two emission scenarios: A2 and B2. Also included dispersal scenarios.	2011-2040, 2041-2070, and 2071-2100
Meyer and others 1999	National — U.S.	Hydrological systems (freshwater)	Identifies elements at greatest risk of impact	Review of published analysis of climate effects on goods and services provided by freshwater ecosystems. Specifically address climate changes, water withdrawal, species invasions, and land use.	na
Munson and others 2012	Local — Sonoran Desert: National Park lands in southern Arizona	Plant species and functional types	Identifies species/groups that will undergo greatest change	Historical trend analysis—100 years' worth of vegetation monitoring. Climate data obtained from weather stations and plant data obtained from surveys.	na
Neilson and others 1998	National — U.S.	Plant communities (habitat)	Measures greatest change	Biogeochemical models: MAPSS and BIOME3. Transient GCM projections. Only considers runoff/soil moisture and has expectations regarding persistence.	2100
Notaro and others 2012	Regional — SW U.S.	Plant functional type, species, biodiversity (trees and shrubs)	Identifies species, plant types, and areas that will experience greatest change	Combined bioclimatic envelope and dynamic vegetation modeling approaches. MaxEnt (BCE modeling) and Lund-Potsdam-Jena (LPJ) DGVM applied to 170 woody species. Biodiversity is also estimated by summing BCE results for each cell. Uses both fixed and elevated CO_2 values in simulations.	1970-2100
Ojima and Lackett 2000	National — U.S.	Comprehensive	Compiles data regarding effects	First part of a larger effort to assess future impacts.	na

Table 5.2. Continued.

Source	Scale	Location	Emphasis	Method	Tools/Measures	Time frame or conditions
Ojima and Lackett 2002	Regional	Western U.S.	Comprehensive	Identify areas of greatest change/impact	Second part of a larger effort to assess future impacts. Vegetation impacts gained through VEMAP and based upon historical and GCM data.	Historical, 2025-2034, 2090-2099
Peery and others 2012	Regional	SW U.S.	Owls	Identifies populations/areas that will experience greatest mortality	Linked observed vital rates (survival) and weather variables using program MARK. Future climate under four GCMs (CNRM-CM3, SCIRO-Mk3.0, ECHam5, MIROC3.2) and three emission scenarios.	1961-1990, 2041-2060, and 2081-2100
Steinke and others 2012 from Furniss and others 2012	Regional	Western U.S.	Watersheds	Identifies watersheds that will have the greatest vulnerability to climate change	Contains 11 case studies from National Forests in the West. Each case study has unique methods for estimating vulnerability. Within the Coconino (Arizona), vulnerability was a function of exposure (e.g., change to snowpack), water value, and watershed sensitivity (e.g., inherent biodiversity).	2030 and 2070
Theobald and others 2010	Regional	Western U.S.	Hydrological systems (watersheds)	Quantifies vulnerabilities for riparian ecosystems	Created a "riparian threats score" integrating info from three-prong analysis. Models of runoff and sediment yield. Used three GCMs under A1B and B1 scenarios.	na
Williams and others 2010	Regional	SW U.S.	Plant species (Trees)	Identifies habitats and species that will undergo greatest change and have highest vulnerability to mortality due to fire/pests	Analyzes historic disturbance trends. Statistical models of tree growth and four scenarios of future climate: A2, A1B, and linear trends established from previous 30 and 144 years.	2050-2099
Winter 2000	National	U.S.	Hydrological (landscape)	Identifies types of hydrological systems most vulnerable to climate change	Assesses characteristics of hydrological landscapes by using the hydrologic-landscape concepts.	na
Zack and others 2010	Regional	Great Plains	Animal species	Quantifies species traits/vulnerability index	NatureServe's Climate Change Vulnerability Index	Three time periods

5.3 Southwest Vulnerability Assessments

Our search identified 36 vulnerability assessments published over the last 17 years addressing climate change in the SW (Table 5.2). These assessments span spatial scales ranging from the local/state level through national, continental, and global ranges (Tables 5.2, 5.3). Two global assessments (Foden and others 2008; Gonzales and others 2010), though not specific to the SW, relate to species sensitivity and adaptive capacity to climate change that has relevance for SW animal species and plant functional types (Table 5.4). Two studies focused on the western hemisphere (Lawler 2009, 2010) and, though broadly focused, provide some insight as to future areas of concern for animal biodiversity. One continental assessment focused on North American animal species (McKenney and others 2007). A large number of assessments (10) focused at the national scale (Tables 5.2, 5.3, 5.4) and most specifically addressed species or habitats (6 of 10) found within the SW. Of the 12 regionally focused assessments, 6 centered on the SW, 3 were more generally focused on the West, and 3 focused on specific habitats: the Great Plains, which includes some of New Mexico and Texas, and the Mojave and Sonoran Deserts, which includes Arizona, California, and Nevada. Of those assessments that dealt with water, 2 were conducted at the national level, 5 were regionally based (Furniss and others 2012 contained cases studies from 11 National Forests), and 1 each focused specifically within New Mexico and the Colorado River Basin (Table 5.3). Two analyses assessed plants and animals within New Mexico (Enquist and others 2008; Enquist and Gori 2008), one assessed plants (Kupfer and other 2005), and two assessments (Coe and others 2012; Friggens and others 2013) considered animal vulnerability and animal and plant vulnerability (Bagne and Finch 2012; Bagne and Finch 2013) at locales within states.

Assessment targets cover biological scales ranging from species to communities for both plants and animals (Table 5.4). Ecosystem-level analyses are quite common in our assessment pool and invariably dealt with habitat changes. One of the published studies (Peery and others 2012) addressed vulnerability at the level of populations. Eight assessments focused on vertebrate animal species, 11 dealt with plant species, and seven dealt with both animal and plant species.

Several common themes were found among SW assessments and climate-related studies:

- Vulnerability of grasslands to invasive species is likely to increase under climate change (Morgan and others 2008; Chambers and Pellan 2008; Neilson and others 1998).
- Changes to hydrological systems include:
  - Higher water temperatures with multiple effects for temperature-dependent species (Johnson and others 2005; Eaton and Scheller 1996).
  - Changes in precipitation events leading to less snowpack, changes to the timing of flood regimes, less flow, and reduced water tables (Theobald and others 2010).
  - Expansion of invasive species in both aquatic and riparian habitats (Theobald and others 2010; Rood and Conrad 2008).
- Many studies show that temperature alone drives or is sufficient to lead to observed or predicted changes (Williams and others 2010, tree growth; Currie 2001, biodiversity; Garfin and Lenart, 2007; Eaton and Scheller 1996, loss of cool water fish species; Meyers and others 1999, many effects on aquatic systems; Hansen and others 2001, plant and animal species richness; Notaro and

others 2012, plant species distributions; a notable exception is cheatgrass invasion, see Bradley 2009).

- Areas near ecotones are more vulnerable to change (Kupfer and others 2005 [in Appendix 2], Madrean habitats; Joyce and others 2008, Biomes; Allen and Breshears 1998).
- Future temperature projections often exceed historic observed maxima, limiting our ability to project future change to biotic species and communities based on bioclimatic modeing (Currie 2001; Williams 2001).

The following discussion compares assessments along a biological spectrum, first describing species-level analyses and moving through community to ecosystem-level analyses. Analyses of hydrological systems are unique and are discussed in their own section. Finally, we discuss assessments that comprehensively address animals, plants, and water.

Table 5.3. Number of assessments focused on animal, plant, or both types of organisms and the various scales presented in 36 assessments of climate change vulnerability for the SW.

	Animal	Both	Plants	Water	Grand total
Global	1		1		2
West Hemisphere	2				2
Continental (North America)			1		1
National	1	4	3	2	10
North America	1				1
U.S.		4	3	2	9
Regional	2	2	3	5	12
Great Plains	1				1
Rocky Mountains				1	1
Sonoran and Mojave Desert			1		1
SW U.S.	1	1	2	2	6
Western U.S.		1		2	3
State (New Mexico only)		1		1	2
State/Local	3				5
MRG, New Mexico	1				1
Sky Islands, Arizona	1		1		2
DoD lands, Southern Arizona		2			2
Local			1	1	2
Colorado River Basin				1	1
Sonoran Desert: National Park lands in southern Arizona			1		1

Table 5.4. Spatial and biological scale of 36 climate change vulnerability assessments conducted for the SW United States. Landscape here refers to studies that address composition of multiple communities across a large area (e.g., North America).

	Animal	Plants				Both				Water			Grand total
	Species	Species	Habitat	Species, ecosystem	Ecosystem	Species	Species, habitat, ecosystem	Habitat	Ecosystem	Hydrological system	Ecosystem	Watershed	
Global	1		1										2
Western Hemisphere	2												2
Continental		1											1
National	1	1			2	1	1	1	1	1		1	10
Regional	2	1	1	2			1			1		4	12
State									1			1	2
State/local	2		1			2							5
Local			1								1		2
Grand total	8	3	3	3	2	3	2	2	1	2	1	6	36

5.3.1 Vulnerability of Southwestern Species and Communities

Species-level assessments are useful for efficiently assessing species of conservation concern. When applied to many species within a taxonomic group or across numerous species in a target area, these methods can also inform management of regional levels of biodiversity. These approaches are most useful when they are used to supply spatially explicit effects of climate change on biodiversity. Of those studies that consider species, we discuss eight that addressed animals and five that considered plants.

Animals

Buckley (2008) used a dynamic biophysical model to assess relative vulnerability of Sceloporus lizards to climate change. Though broad in its analysis, this study showed changes in lizard distributions, including eastward shifts for many species under climate change. This analysis only considers a single aspect of vulnerability (impact), but the author tied these results into a discussion of future trends for lizard conservation. Ultimately, lizards appear quite resilient to the direct effects of warming trends, although it is not clear from this analysis how smaller-scale issues (e.g., interactions, dispersal ability, and plant species change) will influence future lizard distributions.

In a larger-scale analysis, Foden and others (2008) used quantification of traits to measure vulnerability of three animal groups: birds, amphibians, and corals. Foden and others (2008) generated comprehensive lists of species traits indicative of vulnerability that inspired later assessment tools such as NatureServe's climate change index (Young and others 2010) and the SAVS system (Bagne and others 2011). The authors determined 35% of bird species across the globe possess traits that make them potentially sensitive to climate change. Specialized habitat or microhabitat climates and limited dispersal capacities were considered the most problematic issues. The taxonomic group with the greatest number of vulnerable species was the thrush (Turdidae) family, whereas cuckoos (Cuclidae), woodpeckers (Picidae), and doves and pigeons (Columbidae) were the least threatened. A greater proportion (52%) of amphibians than birds was considered vulnerable to future climate changes. Many species were from families not found within the SW. An exception is the Bufonidae family (toads and true toads), which had more than 50% of its species considered susceptible to climate change. Within the Caecilians only 18% of species were considered vulnerable though the authors note this might be due to a lack of information. Traits associated with amphibian vulnerability, including specialized habitat requirements, exclusive occurrence or reliance on threatened or unbuffered aquatic habitats, and dispersal issues related to barriers created by unsuitable habitats were most relevant to amphibians living the in the SW.

Lawler and others (2009) used a consensus based BCE model (see Chapter 3) to assess the effects of climate change as simulated by 10 GCMs under 3 emission scenarios (B1, A1B, and A2) on the range of 1818 birds, 723 mammals, and 413 amphibians across the western United States. In addition to the basic BCE analysis, they compared results of analyses that assumed no dispersal versus unlimited dispersal and calculated a species turnover measure that represented degree of change in species composition. For the majority of climate scenarios (80%), Lawler and others' (2009) analysis showed a loss of 11 and 17% for all species under B1 and A1 scenarios, respectively. Of importance to the SW, Lawler and others (2009) estimated that the greatest turnover for all taxa will occur in mountainous regions and that amphibians are most likely to experience range contractions and loss. In a second analysis focused on amphibians, Lawler and others (2010) combined distribution analysis with data on range limits and expected moisture changes across the western hemisphere to specifically identify sensitive species and areas prone to species loss under climate change. They identified vulnerability according to an index generated by the number of times certain conditions exist within an area. Specifically, one score was given for each of these conditions: (1) area has an estimated turnover (species loss and gain) of at least a 50%; (2) area contains at least 50% range restricted species; and (3) at least 20% of grid cells within the area are projected to experience decreases in precipitation. Their analysis showed that the warm deserts of the United States were projected to have high vulnerability due to decreased precipitation and high species turnover (potential vulnerability of 2 on a scale of 0-3).

Zack and others (2010) examined several species native to the Great Plains region using the Natureserve's Climate Change Vulnerability Index (CCVI, Young and others 2010). They found none of the 30 species ranked in their assessment fell within the highest vulnerability class. Zack and others (2010) did find the Lesser-prairie chicken, regal fritallary, and black-footed ferret moderately vulnerable to climate change effects. Overall, the authors concluded that climate change is not a driving negative force for many species and most species were presumed stable. Zack and others (2010) also examined range location relative to the study site (the Great Plains Landscape Conservation Cooperative) but did not draw additional conclusions regarding species vulnerability.

Four other assessments (Bagne and Finch 2012, 2013; Coe and others 2012; Friggens and others 2013) focused on vertebrate animal species with another vulnerability scoring system, SAVS (Bagne and others 2012). Coe and others (2012) focused on species in southern Arizona and specifically across the Sky Island region. Species were selected based upon criteria set forth by USDA Forest Service Region 3 biologists and included species of conservation and management concern. Riparian associated birds (elegant trogon, western yellow-billed cuckoo) and amphibians (Tarahumara frog, Chiricauhua leopard frog) were among the highest scoring species. Arid adapted species such as the desert tortoise, mesquite mouse, desert bighorn sheep, and Slevin's bunchgrass lizard were the least vulnerable. Coe and others (2012) also provided a comprehensive review of climate projections and evidence for future effects of climate warming trends within the region. Bagne and Finch (2012, 2013) examined species inhabiting two Department of Defense (DoD) installations in Southwestern Arizona (Fig. 5.2). This study was focused on Threatened, Endangered and At-risk species including 21 animals and 2 plants from Ft. Huachuca and 15 animals and 1 plant from Barry M. Goldwater Range (Bagne and Finch 2012, 2013). Their findings suggest that many already threatened species are at risk of additional issues due to climate change. The northern Mexican garter snake, southwest willow flycatcher and Arizona tree frog were the most vulnerable, whereas the Desert massagauga, aplomado falcon, and black-tailed prairie dog were the least vulnerable on Fort Huachuca. Both plant species, the Lemmon fleabane and Huachuca water umbel, received scores indicating increased vulnerability under climate change. For the Barry M. Goldwater Range, the Sonoran pronghorn was the highest scoring species followed by the desert tortoise and cactus ferruginous pygmy owl. The desert bighorn was moderately vulnerable while the California leaf-nosed bat, gilded flicker, and saddled leaf-nosed snake were least vulnerable. Friggens and others (2013) examined 117 species inhabiting the Middle Rio Grande of New Mexico. The species list included both common and rare species that inhabited the riparian corridor of the study area. Their results show many common species have higher vulnerability scores than rare species. In part, this pattern is explained by the natural division between riparian dependent species and those that use the riparian corridor more opportunistically. Within amphibians, frogs (northern leopard frog, western chorus frog) were most vulnerable and spadefoot toads the least vulnerable. Within reptiles, the Great Plains skink and gartersnakes (followed by aquatic turtle species) were the most vulnerable, whereas the rattlesnakes (western diamond back and prairie), kingsnake, and desert grassland whiptail were the least vulnerable. Riparian obligate birds such as the southwest willow flycatcher and the common yellowthroat were the most vulnerable to future changes, whereas the brown-headed cowbird and greater roadrunner were least vulnerable. Within the mammals, the New Mexican meadow jumping mouse and hoary bat received the highest scores whereas the jackrabbit and desert shrew appeared to be the least vulnerable.

Peery and others (2012) conducted a risk analysis that predicted survival and reproduction for three spotted owl (*Strix occidentalis*) populations in the SW (including California). Their analyses show that growing season precipitation (Arizona and New Mexico populations), nesting season temperature (New Mexico), annual precipitation, and minimum nesting season temperatures (Arizona and California) explained most of the observed variation in reproductive status. Survival was positively associated with previous year's precipitation (previous two years in California) and negatively associated with growing season temperature (New Mexico, Arizona). Population projections show rapid declines for owls residing in New Mexico and Arizona under warming trends, whereas Southern Californian populations remain more stable. Peery and others (2012) also assessed potential effects of increased weather variation by doubling variations in precipitation and temperature changes but found little additional effect. For New Mexico and Arizona, populations are already predicted to be nearly extinct by the end of the century so additional decreases in survival rates due to increased variability had little effect on outcome. Southern Californian populations were little affected by projected weather changes whether those projections showed high variability

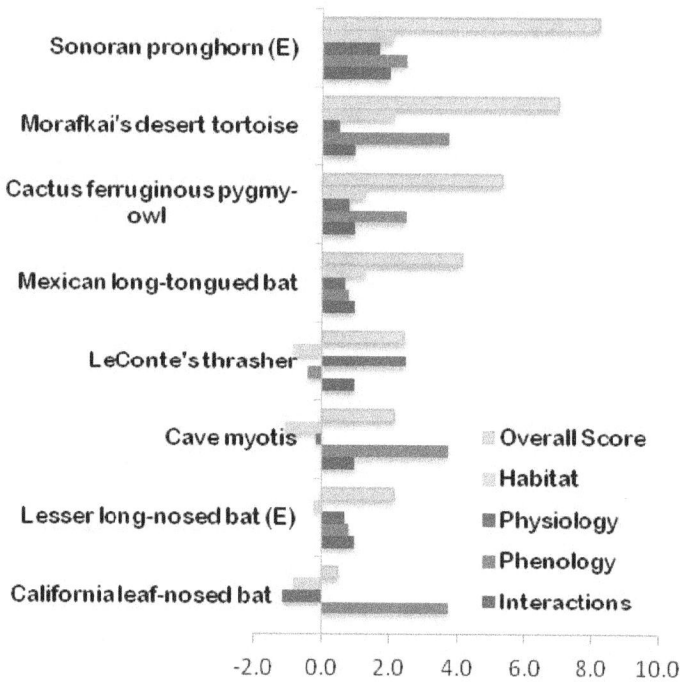

Figure 5.2. Vulnerability of species from the Barry M. Goldwater Range (from Bagne and Finch 2013). This study used a vulnerability index tool that assessed exposure, sensitivity, and adaptive capacity through scenario building and a questionnaire that results in scoring system. Scores were generated for four categories as well as for the collective (overall) expected vulnerability.

or not. It appears that the distinction between southern California populations and New Mexico and Arizona populations reflect the current weather related population trends. Cold, wet springs limit reproductive success in northern California and Oregon populations, and these conditions are likely to decrease with climate warming potentially to the benefit of southern California populations as well. Owls in Arizona and New Mexico are more strongly affected by reductions in prey as a result of drying and warming trends. In addition, temperature increases are likely to be more important drivers than precipitation changes of population trends for owls in Arizona and New Mexico because predicted increases in temperature far exceed norms in annual variation: temperatures increase 3-fold whereas precipitation decreases 1-fold.

Plants

Five studies considered impacts to plant species under warming conditions: the distribution of trees across North America (McKenney and others 2007) and within the SW (Williams and others 2010), the distribution of Sonoran desert plants (Munson and others 2012), and of shrubs and trees (Notaro and others 2012) and invasive grasses (Bradley 2009) in the SW.

McKenney and others (2007) used a climate envelope approach (see Chapter 3) to model the species-environment relationship for 130 North American tree species. Though little is said about the SW, it is interesting to note that projections for the southern United States fall outside of known historical ranges, highlighting a potential issue affecting management planning in the region.

Bradley (2009) provided a measure of risk for invasion from *Bromus* spp. in the western United States, which, while not technically a vulnerability measure (see Chapters 1 and 4), will undoubtedly be important determinant of vulnerability for many native species and ecosystems. The author found that decreased precipitation, particularly in the summer, led to an expansion of up to 45% of suitable habitat for *Bromus*. Increased precipitation was associated with reductions in suitable habitat by as much as 70%. This study is interesting in that identified precipitation as an important if not primary element determining future suitability for invasive *Bromus* spp., in contrast to many other modeling efforts. There are also interesting implications for future *Bromus* spp. spread because precipitation patterns are likely to vary across the Great Plains with increases to the north and decreases to the south. As noted by Bradley (2009), many others have modeled invasive species (Beerling 1993 [Europe]; Sutherst 1995 [IUCN]; Zavaleta and Royval 2002 [Appendix 1]; Kriticaos and others 2003 [Australia]; Mika and others 2008). Among these, Zalaleta and Royval (2002) and Mika and others (2008) provide important discussions regarding the risk of existing habitats to future invasion or expansion of exotic species (Appendix 2). Zavaleta and Royval (2002), in particular, provide information and predictions for plant and animals species that are relevant to the United States though outside our study region.

Williams and others (2010) focused specifically on *Pinus* (*P. edulis* and *P. ponderosa*) species and *Pseudotsuga menziesii* (Douglas-fir) within the West. Williams and others (2010) used statistical models of tree growth based upon tree ring data to estimate growth under future conditions. They also explored contrasts between wildfire and tree mortality due to beetles over a two-decade period to evaluate trends and magnitude of disturbance effect. This analysis projects that the greatest and most widespread decreases in growth will occur in the SW and Colorado Rockies. Their findings also point to the influence of temperature on these observations; SW ponderosa pine and Douglas-fir are likely to be at greatest risk for drought induced mortality at lower level elevations, whereas pinyon pine appears sensitive throughout its range.

Munsen and others (2012), used historic data for plant species and communities types to produce information regarding relative vulnerability among the study species. Using 100 years of vegetation monitoring, the authors described population trends in response to recent changes in climate for Sonoran Desert habitats. They then extrapolated these findings to expectations for future trends in plant species composition. In mesic mesquite savanna, perennial grasses declined with declining precipitation, cacti increased, and *Prosopis velutina* declined in response to increased mean annual temperature. In xeric upland areas, leguminous *Cercidium microphyllum* declined in hillslopes and *Fouquieriea spledens* decreased on south and west facing slopes in response to increasing mean annual temperature. In xeric shrublands, *Larrea tridetata* and hemiparasite *Krameria Grayi* decreased with decreasing cool season precipitation and increasing aridity.

Notaro and others (2012) conducted a comprehensive analysis of future plant distributions for the SW United States that includes New Mexico Arizona, Colorado, and Utah. Their analysis is presented here because it represents valuable information regarding future changes with relevance to the assessment of plant vulnerability to climate change though this study is not in and of itself a vulnerability assessment. Similar studies exist (Bachelet and others 2001; Daly and others 2000; Thompson and others 1998; Shafer and others 2001; Rehfeldt and others 2006) that represent early versions of this type of analysis, which are not reviewed here but are listed in Appendix 2. Notaro and others (2012) simulated future distributions of 170 tree and shrub species. Their analysis compared 14 GCMS under the A2 emission scenario. Using Maxent (Table 3.2), Notaro and others (2012) identified three important predictors of future range of North American species: temperature (with precipitation changes modifying patterns driven by warming trends), growing degree days, and annual mean temperature. Their analysis showed that 83 species will experience a shift northward in ideal conditions, whereas 32 species are expected to shift southward. Overall, 76 species will experience range expansions and 70 species will experience range contractions. For species with the most robust results (agreement between 12 and 14 of the 14 GCMs used), the authors found 29 species with expected increases in range, whereas 39 were expected to experience range contractions, indicating that declines may be more frequent. Two species, Engelmann spruce (*Picea engelmannii*) and Mesquite (*Prosopis juliflora*), were well modeled by current climate conditions and represent plants limited by either high or low temperatures, respectively. Engelmann spruce is a cold tolerant, high elevation, evergreen conifer and the most abundant tree species in the SW (Notaro and others 2012), and mesquite, a drought tolerant tree/shrub, is found in the hotter regions. The distribution of Englemann spruce is expected to decline in the SW, whereas mesquite is likely to expand and shift northward, with the greatest changes seen for those scenarios that predict both warming and drying. Among evergreen species, Tumey oak (*Quercus toumeyi*) and Pringle Manzanita (*Arctostaphylos pringlei*), showed the largest predicted increase in range, whereas limber pine (*Pinus flexilis*) and big sage brush (*Artemisia tridentate*) had the largest projected range contractions. For deciduous species, the greatest expansions were seen for Tracy's hawthorn (*Crataegus tracyi*) and Knowlton's hophornbeam (*Ostrya knowltonii*), and the greatest contractions were seen for Willow hawthorn (*Crataegus saligna*) and narrow leaf cottonwood (*Populus angustifolia*). Climate changes are predicted to lead to an expansion of all yucca species and a majority of the oak species but contractions in most pine species, including ponderosa pine (*Pinus ponderosa*).

Community-level assessments

Analyses based on plant species often form the basis of community level assessments of climate change impacts on habitat (see MAPSS in Chapter 2). From our review, we found three assessments that consider community response as derived from analysis of species, each using quite different methods to measure future vulnerability. One assessment considered plant species and communities and the implication for animal species (Hansen and others 2001), one study (Currie 2001) examined patterns of biodiversity for both plants and animals, and one study focused on the impact of climate changes on distributions of plant groups (Kupfer and others 2005).

Hansen and others (2001) provided the most comprehensive assessment. Their report is broken in two parts: one models vegetation and biodiversity change under three different GCMs, and a second synthesis draws together current knowledge of interactions among climate, land use, and biodiversity with the distribution analysis to discuss future biodiversity and provide strategies and future research needs. Hansen and others (2001) used 4 biodiversity models: MAPSS (biogeographic approach) for biomes, DISTRIB (statistical regression tree) for tree species/forest community type, response surface model (statistical local regression) for tree/shrub species, and Currie (statistical) models for species richness of trees, mammals, birds reptiles, and amphibians. Though their efforts are based upon climate parameters generated from early and now obsolete GCMs, their results identify a number of interesting trends. Statistical regression methods for individual species show that suitable habitat for ponderosa pine is likely to expand westward, whereas sagebrush (*Artemesia*), mountain hemlock, and Engelmann spruce will experience decreases in suitable habitat. MAPSS results showed alpine habitat all but disappears, whereas shrublands and arid woodlands expand into grasslands of the Interior West and Great Plains. The same models predict grasslands expansion into the deserts of the SW. Analysis of community richness revealed a strong correlation of richness with temperature but not precipitation. For trees, species richness is positively related to temperature up to a threshold where the relationship becomes negative. Importantly, richness in SW deserts is expected to decline as conditions get hotter and drier. Endotherms are expected to increase in northern (cooler) areas and experience moderate decreases in warmer areas, whereas ectotherms show monotonic increases along a latitudinal gradient from northern to southern areas. The authors noted great variability in results across GCMs.

Kupfer and others (2005) created predictive models of plant community distributions under 36 different scenarios of temperature and precipitation change with the intent to identify the most sensitive areas within the Sky Island region of southern Arizona. The authors focused on four dominant ecotones: desert scrub, desert grassland, Madrean evergreen woodland, and montane conifer. Increased temperatures alone were predicted to increase desert scrub habitat and lead to upslope movement of most other habitat types. Downslope movements were observed under scenarios of higher precipitation, indicating a high degree of moisture limitation in this system. Desert scrub and montane conifer habitats experienced greater than 50% change in area. However, these patterns could be partially attributed to their limited distribution in the lower and upper reaches of the Sky Islands, respectively, and to the current low abundance values, which led to relatively dramatic changes. In their assessment of vulnerability, Madrean evergreen classes and areas near ecotones were most sensitive and showed the greatest change in area with change in climate variables.

Currie (2001) used bioenergetics approaches to estimate future changes in biodiversity and predicted significant declines in tree, bird and mammal species in the SW. Currie's predictions were based upon relationships between maximum July temperature and biodiversity, which appear to be closely linked. Species richness increased with increasing temperature though eventually reached a plateau and fell (decreases) as temperatures continued to rise. Importantly, Currie noted, as did Williams (2001), that projections for the SW often exceed the hottest observed July temperature predictions and, therefore, these models may underestimate the true effect of temperature increases on species richness in the SW.

Results of Notaro and others (2012) bioclimate analysis (see previous section) were used to estimate shifts in biodiversity across the region. They predicted major declines in high elevation evergreen forests, especially in Utah and Colorado, as well as Sonoran desert habitat but expected some level of enhancement to biodiversity of prairie ecosystems of eastern New Mexico. Changes to high elevation species appeared to be driven mostly by increases in mean July temperature, and the Sonoran desert species appear to be most sensitive to projected January temperatures. Interestingly, drier hotter conditions were predicted to favor diversity in New Mexico grasslands by providing an environment conducive to the establishment of Sonoran or Chihuahuan desert habitat, which are relatively species rich.

Animal species of the southwestern United States

Though a number of important areas of concern were noted for species inhabiting the SW, results from species-level vulnerability assessments were generally not comparable because they lack broad applicability. There were no instances where a single species was assessed by more than one of the studies reviewed here in a way that allows direct and meaningful comparisons. However, we did find a tendency for riparian associated species to be among the highest ranking or most vulnerable species within each assessment (Bagne and Finch 2012, 2013; Coe and others 2012; Friggens and others 2013). In addition, lizard species were not found to be particularly vulnerable to climate change effects where they were studied

(Buckley 2008; Friggens and others 2013). Peery and others (2012) was the only study to model survival and reproduction for three SW sites, and their analysis showed important regional differences relating to current limiting conditions (cold versus dry weather).

Species-level studies covered a variety of spatial scales (Tables 5.3, 5.4). Foden (2008) examined species across their range and made general conclusions about taxonomic group vulnerability that did not consider local-level influences. Peery and others (2012) examined three owl populations in three states and found distinct differences in predictions across the region but also recognized that their predictions for local extinctions may not reflect trends at larger scales. Buckley considered lizard distributions at the national level, and Bagne and Finch (2012, 2013), Coe and others (2012), and Friggens and others (2013) created ranks based on local-level responses to predict future population trends for species inhabiting specifically defined areas. Though information gathered from these latter assessments could be applied to other populations, issues noted for a specific region cannot be extrapolated to new regions without careful consideration. However, smaller-scale assessments that address specific species within their current habitats provide information that is highly relevant to managers. In addition, fine-scale analyses of species of specific concern or inhabiting areas of management interest are likely to be necessary for most management plans.

The focal target of each vulnerability assessment varied with important implications for the interpretation of assessment results. The ranking reported in Foden (2008) compliments the results found for the MRG bird study (Friggens and others 2013) but differs somewhat from Bagne and Finch (2012, 2013) and Coe and others (2012). The latter assessments focus on species already of concern, a status related to life history traits (e.g., specialization and sensitivity to habitat loss) that not only influence population vulnerability to declines but relate, in many cases, to additional vulnerability to climate-related effects.

Most species-level assessments relied on a quantification technique to rank species rather than statistical modeling. In such systems, uncertainty is considered by the user and appended to the output of the ranking typically as a separate associated value. This measure of uncertainty addresses data gaps and the general confidence in methods that model climate and habitat change. Foden (2008) indicated high levels of data insufficiency for amphibians. Coe and others (2012), Bagne and Finch (2012; 2013), and Friggens and others (2013) identified species and areas that require more research as related to species information, but do not estimate uncertainty related to climate modeling or other estimates of exposure. For Peery and others (2012), who did use a statistical model, uncertainty relates to variation in climate projections and the complex relationship between environmental change and population size. For instance, behavioral avoidance mechanisms like seeking cool roosts or shifting ranges northward are expected to prevent overall extinction of owls.

Plant species and community data

Within the studies that considered plant species and communities, estimates and predictions of future responses relied mostly on modeled projections relating either growth or habitat suitability to climate conditions. As with animal species, variations in scale and targets of the various assessments limit generalized conclusions for the SW. However, trends for species and communities tended to compliment on another. In general, tree species did well until reaching a temperature threshold beyond which trees and forested habitats are expected to decline. These patterns are more evident for high altitude areas, where temperature thresholds are generally lower, and for low elevation areas in the hottest part of New Mexico and Arizona. In particular, Engelmann spruce was predicted to experience declines in suitable habitat in multiple assessments. Interestingly, at a national level, SW forests are not expected to be the most vulnerable to climate change relative to other North American habitats. Still, at a smaller spatial scales, it is evident that tree species will undergo significant changes in habitat suitability as a result of climate change. Changes to forest systems may have wide reaching implications as the composition of these systems affect biogeochemistry and hydrological processes.

An important implication of these plant studies, particularly at those that look at the collective response of species to increasing temperatures (Hansen and others 2001; Currie 2001) is the notion that there is a threshold effect where either species do well (e.g., richness increases) up to a certain temperature level or species within a region do well provided conditions are not already near a particular temperature limit. There are areas that may experience increases in biodiversity as warmer temperatures extend growing seasons and lead to range expansions of species and biomes (e.g. northward shifts of Sonoran and Chihuahuan deserts). Alternatively, areas that already experience hot and dry conditions (e.g., the SW) may experience temperatures beyond the tolerances of many native species. Ultimately, changes in biodiversity will vary across the landscape with variations in preexisting species and communities and the exact nature of temperature and precipitation changes.

5.3.2 Vulnerability of Southwestern Habitats

Neilson and others (1998) provided the earliest estimates for species composition change. In their national assessment, they compared MAPSS and BIOME3 results under a variety of projections and assessed habitat change based on transient GCMs. These early climate projections are less xeric than those produced by later models. Perhaps the most interesting result of this analysis is their projection for an overall increase in Leaf Area Index (LAI, commonly used as a measure of productivity) in direct response to increased CO_2. Though their predictions do not consider other factors commonly known to limit LAI, and are projected for a somewhat mesic future, these results are reflected in later analyses. Joyce and Birdsey (2000) took a different approach and presented a comparative analysis of trends and impacts of climate change on America's forest communities (Fig. 5.3). This extensive report contains several chapters that outline major biomes shifts under various climate projections, addresses ecosystem productivity, and discusses the implications of climate change for carbon budgets as well as the forest sector. Bachelet and Neilson (2000) compared multiple simulations generated through MAPSS, BIOME2 and BIOME3, and DOLY from three distinct studies. Each study was conducted either at a regional or continental scale under varying climate change scenarios. Comparisons among DOLY, BIOME2, and MAPSS using projections from the Fourth Assessment Report (FAR) show a large degree of divergence between models. Ultimately, the results of their comparison showed that the strongest agreement centered on expectation for large decreases in the area of arid lands, which ultimately become grasslands. All models predict a decrease in runoff for all habitat types under all scenarios. However, their comparison also highlights the influence of CO_2 on model performance where notable differences existed for the same model run with and without CO_2 effects. Only two trends were consistent among the model results: where CO_2 inputs were included, all models agreed that shrubland areas decreased; when CO_2 effects were excluded, all models agreed that tundra and alpine habitats decline. MAPSS and BIOME2 simulated loss of boreal forests and increases in savanna and grassland habitat.

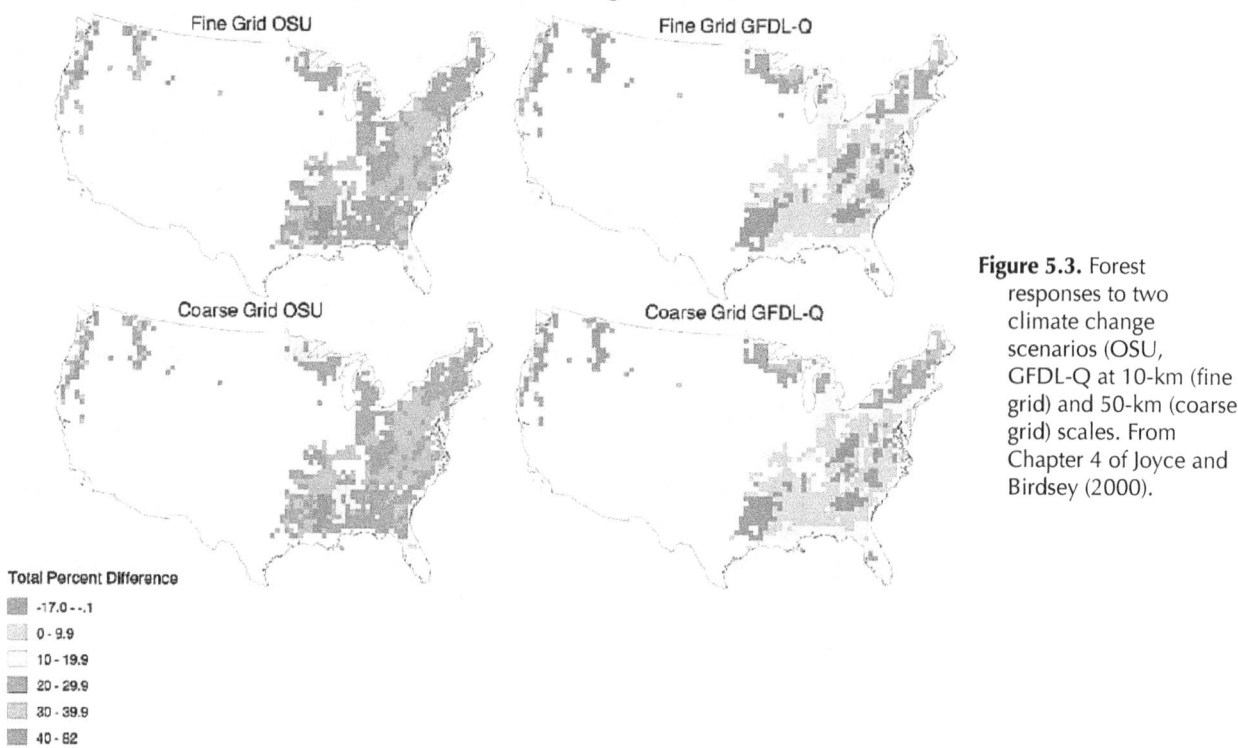

Figure 5.3. Forest responses to two climate change scenarios (OSU, GFDL-Q at 10-km (fine grid) and 50-km (coarse grid) scales. From Chapter 4 of Joyce and Birdsey (2000).

MAPSS also predicted a decrease in temperate forest and increase in savannas and grasslands in direct contrast to predictions by BIOME. With respect to arid lands, both DOLY and MAPSS simulated increases though DOLY produced the greatest increase in southwestern deserts.

Joyce and others (2008) reviewed 50 State Wildlife Action Plans to assess climate change as potential threat to wildlife terrestrial habitats. Using descriptions provided by the wildlife action plans they ranked areas along a gradient of high to low threat via a "climate stress index." The index incorporates information on the degree of expected climate change as well as climate induced shifts in habitat area and quality and expected plant species response based on ecological assumptions regarding the effects of elevated CO_2. Habitat specific analyses were conducted for Arizona, Minnesota, and Tennessee. From 189 studies that document climate related changes, Joyce and others (2008) identified multiple range expansions for mammals in Arizona and New Mexico, one bird phenology change in Arizona, and a single instance of mammal morphological change in New Mexico (Fig. 4.1). The authors also provided a detailed analysis that considers current land use practices, prevalence of at risk species, and expected change in total habitat area. They found that areas of greatest stress are associated with biome transitions zones and areas with high topographic relief. They also noted that areas expected to be most stressed by climate change did not overlap areas currently considered at high risk (due to fragmentation, urbanization, etc.), which might complicate future management priorities. The southern great plains were considered least sensitive according to their stress scale (northern Arizona and New Mexico scored high). Habitat-level analysis showed that species gains and losses were relatively rare events in Arizona though xeric habitats are identified as potential high stress areas. For Arizona, temperate mixed xeromorphic woodlands were considered at risk of complete loss, and the area covered by temperate coniferous forest, tropical thorn woodland, and warm temperate/subtropical mixed savanna is expected to increase. Temperate arid shrublands were among the most stressed habitat types but were also generally rarer.

Enquist (2008) and Enquist and Gori (2008) summarized data for New Mexico regarding climate effects on habitats and watersheds. Both studies are entirely retrospective but use the data to infer future vulnerability and are focused across the entire state of New Mexico. In their first report, Enquist and Gori (2008) used the number of drought sensitive species inhabiting an area and the magnitude of recent climate changes to compare the relative and likely vulnerability of New Mexican habitats. They identified 11 areas potentially vulnerable to climate change. Three areas, the Sierra San Luis/Peloncillo Mountains, the Jemez Mountains, and the southern Sangre de Cristo Mountains, were considered particularly vulnerable. They also identified 10 sites that were less vulnerable. These sites, despite harboring large numbers of drought-sensitive species, experienced lower climate exposure and include Bottomless Lakes, Bitter Lake, and Blue River/Eagle Creek. Sites with few drought sensitive species or little observed change in climate, such as the western plains of San Augustine, the Middle Pecos River, Saldo Creek, and Patura Grasslands, were not considered particularly vulnerable to future climate change.

Gonzales and others (2010) used observed and expected biome distributions to estimate vulnerability. Vulnerability represented a composite of the probability of change in climate and the degree overlap between historic and projected vegetation as generated using MC1 (Gonzales and others 2010). Their findings reinforce the notion that the SW has and will continue to undergo a relatively large change in temperature. At the global scale, temperate shrublands, temperate grassland, and deserts had high fractions of their coverage area within a vulnerable or highly vulnerable classification as determined by measures of observed change. Future projections and degree of overlap between current and future distributions were not substantially different for these habitats, however, and these vegetation communities were not among those considered most vulnerable.

Notaro and others (2012) simulated future changes in plant functional types in the SW using dynamic vegetation modeling. Their analysis, which considered high (A1) and medium (B1) emission scenarios under fixed and increasing (CO_2 enriched) CO_2 for 17 GCMs provides several informative trends. First, vegetation is generally expected to decline. Second, some areas and vegetation types are more likely to experience loss. For example, deciduous forests in Utah and Colorado are expected to undergo the greatest declines. Spatial patterns of vegetation loss corresponded with the greatest expected declines in associated plant types. Grasses were predicted to increase into areas formerly occupied by deciduous trees at lower elevations but trees (evergreens) may expand at higher elevations. Third, regional changes in vegetation cover are influenced differentially by temperature and precipitation changes. Precipitation strongly influenced estimates of vegetation die off, particularly for grasslands. Conversely, tree cover was strongly and inversely correlated to temperature. Fourth, CO_2 enrichment mitigates some of the expected declines in vegetation, especially for grassland habitats (as found for Neilson and other 1998; Joyce and others 2000). Loss of grass cover in the eastern Colorado, New Mexico, and northern Sonaran/Chihuahuan deserts were the most robust trends under fixed CO_2 scenarios. These changes were much smaller under enriched CO_2 conditions.

A more specific assessment was conducted for the Mojave and Sonoran Deserts in Arizona, Nevada, California, and Mexico (Comer and others 2012). Using an index-based system derived from the NatureServe's CCVI (see Appendix 1) for species, Comer and others (2012) integrated estimates of climate exposure, change to disturbance processes, and species distribution models to develop a system for assessing a wide variety of ecosystem or community types. The authors also employed a series of workshops to incorporate expert opinions. For the purpose of their case study, the authors apply this system to 10 focal natural communities and provide estimates of vulnerability due to combined influence of indirect and direct climate change effects as well as adaptive capacity. The assessment is comprehensive and brings together estimates of the degree change in temperature and precipitation from average, climate envelope shift, forecasts of fire and hydrological events, and multiple indicators of current landscape condition as generated from a number of modeling techniques as well as a ranking system to integrate multiple effects into one indicator value. Climate change vulnerability is calculated by generating scores for direct effects, which represents exposure elements (e.g., climate change stress, BCE analysis of habitat change, and forecasts of disturbance processes) and a resilience score, which combines several elements of the indirect effect of climate change (e.g., invasive species, departures from disturbance regimes) as well as inherent characteristics that might lend the ecoregion greater adaptive capacity (e.g., biodiversity, narrow distribution).

Overall, three of eight communities within the Sonoran ecoregion, North American warm desert riparian woodland and stream, North American warm desert mesquite bosque, and Sonora-Mojave creosotebush-white bursage desert scrub had high climate change vulnerability (Comer and others 2012). The remaining communities, desert springs and seeps, Sonaran Palo verde-mixed cacti desert scrub, Sonora-Mojave mixed salt desert scrub, North American warm desert active and stabilized dunes, and Apacherian-Chihuahuan semi-desert grassland were considered moderately vulnerable to climate change. Each of the moderately vulnerable communities was considered highly sensitive to the direct effects of climate change but had a high resilience score, whereas, high vulnerability was associated with highly sensitivity to direct climate change effects but only moderately resilience scores. For the Mojave ecoregion, three of seven community types, Mojave mid-elevation mixed desert scrub, North American warm desert mesquite bosque, and North American warm desert riparian woodland and stream had high overall vulnerability scores (Comer and others 2012). Each of these community types had high sensitivity scores for direct climate effects and moderate resiliency scores. The remaining five community types, Sonora-Mojave mixed salt desert scrub, Sonora-Mohave creosotebush-white bursage desert scrub, Great Basin pinyon-juniper woodland, North American warm desert active and stabilized dunes, and desert springs and seeps were moderately vulnerable to climate change. The Sonora-Mojave mixed salt desert scrub and Sonora-Mohave creosotebush-white bursage desert scrub were moderately sensitive to direct climate effects and moderately and highly resilient, respectively, due to low risks of indirect impacts and generally good adaptive capacity. Great Basin pinyon-juniper woodlands and North American warm desert active and stabilized dunes were considered highly sensitive but also had a high resilience score. Community types received similar ranks across both ecoregions with the exception of Sonora-Mojave creostebush-white Bursage desert scrub, which was given moderate and high vulnerability for the Mojave and Sonoran ecoregions, respectively. Direct impacts of climate change were scored as vulnerable for this habitat within the Sonoran desert ecoregions, which appeared to be driven by less drastic shifts in temperature and precipitation and predicted distribution of this habitat within the Mojave region (see Comer and others 2012).

Summary and discussion: Habitat-level assessments

From the studies conducted for the SW, we found several indications for widespread shifts in many plant functional groups. As with species and community level analyses, most studies show a significant reduction in habitats associated with high elevations but increases in the area suitable for desert grassland and shrubland habitat. Shifts in suitable habitat were evident for most plant functional groups but results were strongly influenced by CO_2, and temperature and precipitation changes with varying results across the SW region. The greatest confidence lies with predictions for expansions northward and up in elevation of most habitats and functional groups.

Studies of suitable habitat were difficult to compare because output targets varying time frames (see Table 5.3) and varying levels of biological organization (plant species versus plant functional groups versus habitat types) and are based upon a large and variable subset of model parameters (see chapter 3, Tables 3.1, 3.2). For instance, the studies conducted for the SW and discussed or incorporated into vulnerability assessments are based on a subset of 12 different GCM outputs, 3 possible emission scenarios, and 8 unique vegetation modeling approaches (Table 5.2). In addition, CO_2 has a strong but variable influence on models and its treatment across the current analyses is not consistent. Joyce and Birdsey (2000) provided the most comprehensive review of model output for a single habitat type—forests. It is clear from this work that the individual needs and expectations of a management problem will be important for identifying the relevance of a particular effort for informing management actions.

Habitat-level vulnerability assessments are useful for predicting impact of climate change on diversity patterns where specific taxonomic group are not well studied or in areas with high species richness (which creates a burden to conducting numerous individual assessments). Large-scale analyses tend to rely on modeling methods, which provide valuable tools to create and compare scenarios. However, the tradeoff in these types of approaches is that they are less suited for generating analyses of well-known taxa and results can be somewhat generalized. In addition, analyses that are done at the scale of a biome may not be able to distinguish between fine-scaled effects and cannot account for changes in community structure. In one example, the effect of reduced tree density on biomass as might occur from diebacks would not be modeled in habitat level studies because these changes do not change biome classification. It has been argued that such broadbrush approaches can lead to underestimations in rate of change (Gonzales and others 2010). Uncertainty is also harder to measure and mitigate for these analyses because it is incorporated through statistical means that can be rather obscure to interpret or even notice. Joyce and others (2008) observed variation in stress scores were more closely related to the GCM selected than either emission or ecological scenario assumptions, an interesting observation that reflects the impact of various methodologies.

5.3.3 Vulnerability of Southwestern Water

Water is important to arid regions such as the SW. Riparian systems typically support a disproportionate amount of the regional biodiversity. These systems are also likely to be strongly affected by changes in climate with a concordant disproportionate effect on surrounding landscapes and features (Fig. 5.4). The primary factor understood to determine vulnerability of water systems to climate change is its reliance on atmospheric versus ground water sources. The former are

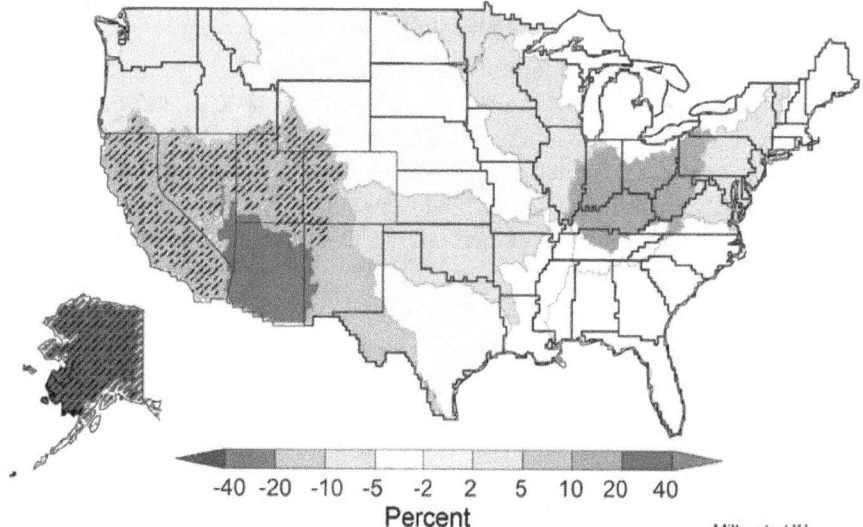

Figure 5.4. Projected changes in median runoff for 2041-2060 as compared to 1901-1970 based on modest emission scenario. Grey lines represent water-resource region. Hatched areas indicate greatest confidence in model projections. From the U.S. Global Change Research Program, 3rd National Climate Assessment.

Milly et al.[151]

generally considered much more prone to issues with respect to changing precipitation regimes. We review nine assessments that consider the future vulnerability of Western or SW riparian and water systems to climate change.

Hauer and others (1997) provided the earliest focus on the Rocky Mountains and discussed biogeochemistry, fluvial characteristics, and the biota of river and lake ecosystems. Specifically, they identified research needs and strategies for dealing with the combined issue and influence of anthropogenic disturbance and climate effects. Their report provides useful information regarding past and more current conditions and hypotheses about future climate conditions with a particular focus on the relationship to hydrological and biological processes.

Meyer and others (1999) reviewed climate assessments conducted for freshwater systems across the United States in an attempt to gauge effects on goods and services. Though not a typical assessment, this review provides valuable insight as to the implications of climate change on future sustainability and it draws together a body of literature in order to compare the relative vulnerabilities of various regions and systems to climate change. The authors quantify the vulnerability of each region according to the extent of the expected effect and the context of the systems with respect to anthropogenic influences. Notably, these authors suggested that altered patterns of land use, water withdrawal, and species invasions may dwarf or at the very least exacerbate climate change impacts. Their review highlights several specific predictions:

- Shifts in distributions of aquatic insects (Sweeney and others 1992).
- Altered plant assemblages and changes in nutrient cycles (Meyer and Pulliam 1992).
- Changes in sediment load and channel morphology (Ward and others 1992).
- Loss of some fish species (particularly from east-west oriented streams [Carpenter and others 1992]).
- Changes in hydrologic variability (e.g., the frequency or magnitude and seasonality of storm or flood events) may have a greater impact on aquatic systems than long-term changes in means.
- Vulnerability has different sources depending upon the system. For wetlands, changes in water balance increase vulnerability to fire and changes to greenhouse gas exchanges are the largest consequence. Streams will be more heavily

influenced by impacts on the riparian zone, species-specific thermal tolerances, and changes in flow regime.

Meyer and others (1999) identified the Arctic, Great Lakes, and Great Plains (particularly the prairie potholes) as vulnerable to climate change effects. For the Rocky Mountains, warmer temperatures are likely to lead to fragmentation of cold water fish habitat and change aquatic insect distributions. This region is overtly affected by human activities, however, so many of the climate effects may be dwarfed by ongoing issues (Meyer and others 1999). The Great Plains contain a variety of aquatic ecosystems under a strong east-west precipitation gradient. Warming is expected to dramatically influence the form of precipitation and timing of floods. As a result, the Great Plains and Prairie regions of the United States and California are considered particularly vulnerable to climate change. Increased salinity as a result of increases in evaporation rates, especially in the western Great Plains, is a leading factor predicted to lead to loss of endemic fish species, many of which are already near their thermal tolerance limit. The authors also noted that the arid SW should be considered vulnerable to climate effects but that the nature of predicted changes, which have a great deal of uncertainty, prevent accurate assessments. The arid SW is already characterized by its variable and unpredictable weather patterns, which may be one reason why the riparian systems in this region are so sensitive to changes in precipitation and, potentially, temperature. In addition, the isolated nature of many systems increases the vulnerability of endemic species to extinction as a result of climate change. Increases in salinity due to increase evaporation and reduced precipitation may exacerbate the rate of species invasions and lead to widespread changes in riparian structure and food webs (Meyer and others 1999). Interestingly, the authors considered the degree of change in flow components from current conditions to be more important in determining the extent of impact on streams than increased temperature along. Finally, changes to the periodicity of flow (from episodic to perennial or vice versa) are much more likely to result in irreversible changes and reduce ecosystem function in the short term.

In another review, Perry and others (2011) (Table 5.1) identified specific outcomes under a set of assumptions about future stream flow. Specifically, changes in streamflow are expected to reduce the abundance of native early successional species but favor greater herbaceous species and late successional and drought-tolerant woody species. Climate changes will also reduce nutrient cycling and litter decomposition and, in general, decrease habitat quality for many species.

Winter (2000) used hydrological landscapes characteristics to determine climate change vulnerability and concluded that systems that rely primarily on rainwater are the most vulnerable. Specifically, vulnerability is related to the inherent capacity of the system to compensate (through reliance on other water sources) for variation in precipitation variables. This study does not, however, identify specific scenarios of exposure or identify the specific water bodies that are likely to be vulnerable. Rather, this acts as a measure of how and why a hydrological system is vulnerable to climate change, which then can be applied to classify systems. Winter (2000) classified six types of hydrological landscapes. Among these, wetlands in mountainous landscapes, wetlands associated with glacial landscapes and broad interior basins (playas) are predicted to be the most vulnerable. Vulnerability of wetlands in plateaus and high plains and riverine landscapes vary according the degree to which upper and lower regions depend upon precipitation and according to the size of the hydrological systems. Those that rely on precipitation (typical of upland areas) and are small are most vulnerable.

Christensen and Lettenmaier (2006) conducted a quantitative analysis to estimate the implications of future climate change on runoff for the Colorado River Basin. Though not a climate change vulnerability assessment as technically defined, this publication represents a comprehensive modeling effort for their study region and is the first to identify specific outcomes as a result of climate change. Christensen and Lettenmaier (2006) considered output from 11 GCMs under 2 emission scenarios for 3 time periods. Most models predict increased winter precipitation and decreased summer precipitation and all showed substantial declines in runoff. The authors found evapotranspiration had greatest influence on runoff estimates and runoff declines were reflected in reservoir performance, which led to lost reservoir storage and declines in hydropower. The role of evapotranspiration in driving trends in runoff is likely to be important for determining system vulnerability in light of the conclusions of Meyer and others (1999) who argued that the changes in flow regime are most important for determining future condition.

A recent case study for the San Pedro National Conservation area in Southern Arizona, though based on a risk assessment approach, provides detailed information regarding issues related to climate effects for a SW system (Julius and others 2006). The authors evaluated the influence of five climate scenarios on species, vegetation, and habitat suitability and linked vegetation data into ground water and surface water models to characterize evaporation processes. Results were generated by linking climate, hydrology, and ecosystems models to simulate future change and then incorporating land use stressors. They used historic weather data to create transient climate scenarios for the period 2003-2102 and created multiple possible future scenarios that were based on projections provided by SRAG, 2000. Climate change clearly affected riparian communities leading to greater fragmentation of habitats and a transition to more xeric plant communities. Some variability existed for predictions of future recruitment of native species where winter precipitation timing and amount could lead to lower or higher than currently observed recruitment rates. The authors also determined a strong negative effect for avian biodiversity, particularly for currently abundant species.

Hurd and Coonrod (2008) focused within the SW and conducted analysis using models of streamflow and runoff. They also incorporated a land use component and estimated future agricultural and urban water demands. Their analysis shows that peak flow and total stream flow declines across both wetter and drier scenarios. Further, their results suggest increased monsoons will not offset effects of reduced snowpack in headwaters. Finally, over time, they model a pronounced shift to an early peak flow and significant shift in late winter runoff. This leads to greater reliance on reservoirs and aquifers. The southern reaches of the Rio Grande are likely to be more impacted by these effects.

In the second of three reports regarding New Mexico ecosystems, Enquist and others (2008) ranked watersheds in New Mexico according to two measures: magnitude of exposure and biological diversity. Exposure is estimated using climate data generated from the Climate Wizard site, which allows a user to map and analyze long-term trends in climate data. They also combined that information with recent trends in snowpack and water runoff patterns to generate an estimate in moisture stress (identified as a rate or trend). Biodiversity and, in particular, diversity of sensitive species was used as an indicator of importance of each watershed. In addition to important conservation species, Enquist and others (1998) identified species as sensitive if they were reported as a species of greatest conservation need by the New Mexico Department of Game and Fish's State Wildlife Action Plan. In general, lower elevation watersheds have experienced greater drying than high elevation watersheds though about 93% of watersheds overall showed some decrease in moisture availability over the 1970-2006 study periods. In addition, there was a tendency to find more drying at drier watersheds (versus more mesic sites). Some watersheds appeared to experience less drying, primarily in the southeast quadrant of the state, for summer and fall seasons. Enquist and others (1998) found 45 to 109 sensitive species across individual watersheds. Though there were no significant trends overall, they did find a strong and significant relationship between increasing moisture stress and species richness when considering only the most species-rich watersheds. They identified the Jemez Cloverdale and Playas Lake watersheds as the most vulnerable due to the magnitude of observed moisture stress. The Pecos Headwaters, Upper Rio Grande, Upper Gila, and San Francisco watersheds have experienced little moisture stress but are species rich and were identified as potential targets for successful conservation. In their conclusion, Enquist and others noted that changes in climate and hydrology affect species in numerous ways and, within the SW, may be especially important where species face critical thresholds relating to metabolic and reproductive success (noted first in Burkett and others 2005 and Ryan and others 2008). The authors also identified two types of watersheds that should be focused upon: those that were found most vulnerable and those that are less vulnerable but ecologically important due to high levels of biodiversity. This study is particularly useful for summarizing trends specifically within the SW because it supports many of the suppositions of the previous reviews.

Theobald and others (2010) reviewed and analyzed threats to riparian ecosystems in the western United States. Again framed as a risk assessment that formally quantifies (by definition of RAP) risk, sensitivity, resilience, threat and vulnerability of the systems, this study warrants review here. The authors created "riparian threats score" integrating information from a three-prong analysis. They developed three scenarios that classify three system components—longitudinal, upland, and riparian zone—consisting themselves of multiple variables. Using geospatial data, models of runoff and sediment yield were generated and past and future scenarios of climate and land-use change were used to characterize landscape-scale processes influencing riverine and riparian areas. They also integrated two key stressors: urbanization and changes in climate (primarily precipitation). Similar to other analyses and assessments, Theobald and others (2010) expected decreases in flow for Rio Grande region due to increased discharge. However, they also predicted increased flow for Colorado and Great Basin Regions. Still, southern Arizona and New Mexico received very high riparian threats scores. Flow fragmentation was among the worst for watersheds in Arizona and New Mexico though these same watersheds were not among those with the highest degree of modified riparian area. Lower Arizona watersheds are expected to be most heavily impacted by future changes. Southern New Mexico watersheds were considered among those in the worst condition (furthest from natural setting) with respect to future increases in sedimentation. Additional considerations were also noted for riparian systems in the study region. For instance, higher order streams have most severe and widespread modifications (versus lower order). This study designed a broad approach method for scoring systems to identify high scoring riparian areas in need of further investigation at smaller spatial scales.

Most recently, the USDA Forest Service Climate Change Resource Center in collaboration with National Forest conducted a pilot watershed assessment of 11 National Forests (Furniss and others 2012). The primary goal of this assessment was to link and integrate the relatively well known hydrological impacts of climate change with existing programs and policies currently applied to western National Forests. Each participating Forest independently assessed watershed vulnerability under a proposed National Watershed Vulnerability Assessment (WVA) framework that considered aquatic species, water uses, and infrastructure. Of particular interest to the current discussion is the assessment conducted in the Coconino National Forest (Steinke 2012). Using a step-wise approach based on USDA Watershed Analysis (USDA 1994), the authors compared vulnerability among five watersheds. In addition to the three variables of the WVA, Steinke (2012) included values relating to riparian and spring and stream habitats. Each watershed was given a resource value based on the number of sensitive fish and amphibian species, degree of anthropogenic disturbance (roads), and miles of riparian habitat. Exposure estimates of future temperature, precipitation, runoff and snowpack for years 2030 and 2080 were generated using predictions from climate and the Variable Infiltration Capacity models provided by the Climate Impacts Group (CIG). Sensitivity was determined by considering current condition as well as natural sensitivities of watershed to changes in climate and flow parameter. Each element, water value, sensitivity, and exposure was then assessed by the pilot working team and scored as either low, moderate, or high. Composite scores and maps were then generated describing areas by these scoring values (Fig. 5.5). The greatest perceived issue arising from changes in climate dealt with decreased snowpack, to which watersheds above 6400 ft are most likely to be susceptible. In addition, high elevation sites tended to have high resource values and sensitivity scores and were generally found most vulnerable in this assessment. Considerable information is presented on specific results from this assessment in appendices of Furniss and others (2012).

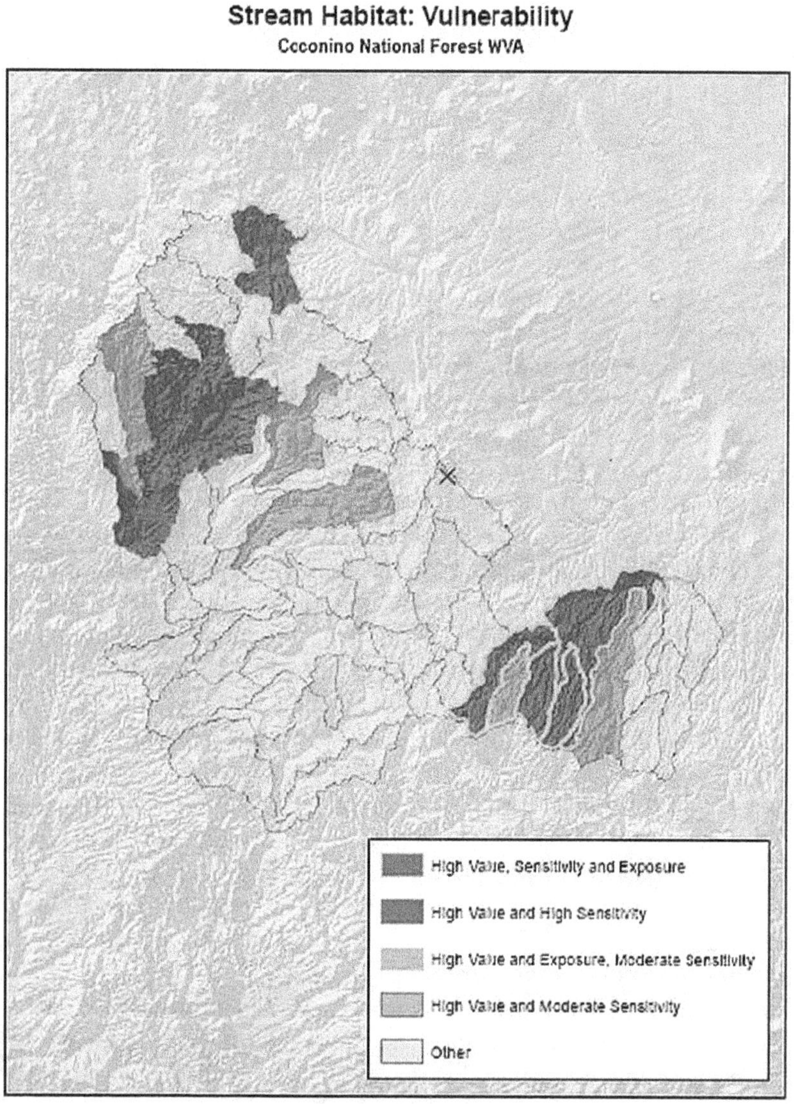

Stream Habitat: Vulnerability
Coconino National Forest WVA

Legend:
- High Value, Sensitivity and Exposure
- High Value and High Sensitivity
- High Value and Exposure, Moderate Sensitivity
- High Value and Moderate Sensitivity
- Other

Figure 5.5. Vulnerability of watershed (blue outline) as estimated by combining scored estimates of water resource values, sensitivity, and exposure.

Summary and discussion: Hydrological systems

It is clear from most assessments, and particularly those focused on SW systems, that there are wide ranging effects for the precipitation driven systems of the SW. Temperature alone drives these changes and precipitation effects are largely a matter of delaying or accelerating the consequences of increased temperatures. Riparian analyses and assessments invariably considered human land use change to determine future vulnerability. It is clear from a review of the literature that riparian and aquatic scientists consider human influences as a critical component of systems. Overall, higher elevation watersheds and those in southern New Mexico and Arizona were considered most vulnerable to climate changes. A cross-site analysis of three U.S. systems showed that the impact of climate change on an individual watershed was largely determined by the extent of its influence on current stressors, which directly relate to human use issues (Julius and others 2006). For the SW, water draw is the primary issue, and many of the assessments (e.g., Hurd and Coonrod 2008) show some reason for concern with respect to future water availability under warming scenarios. In addition, many SW systems rely on hydrological characteristics driven by seasonal precipitation patterns, in particular, winter snow pack. Given the relationship between river flow and riparian habitat, there seems a high probability that western riparian habitats will decline under future warming trends, particularly in the SW.

Scale influences the degree to which SW ecosystems are considered at risk of climate change effects. In their national analysis, Theobald and others (2010) considered SW riparian systems to be in a relatively undegraded state. However, this may be a matter of identifying the lesser of a suite of negative future expectations, and it is clear from their report that the future of these systems under the combined stress of human water use and climate induced changes to the hydrological regime will create substantial issues for species conservation and human consumption.

5.3.4 Comprehensive Assessments

Ojima and Lackett (2000) compiled climate change impact data for the entire United States into an assessment as part of the National Assessment Synthesis Team for the Global Change Research Program Report. This assessment reviewed knowledge and extrapolated information to identify areas of greatest concern. Many of the issues drawn from this report continue to be reflected in the studies and assessments identified in this synthesis of SW climate change vulnerability assessments. Though general in its applicability, this report succinctly summarizes ongoing issues with respect to climate change in the United States.

Ojima and Lackett (2002) assessed future impacts of climate change on both natural and social systems. Though not formatted as a traditional assessment, this report combines several elements that relate to aspects of vulnerability. Ojima and Lackett (2002) employed a stakeholder driven assessment where stakeholders from multiple economic sectors directed analysis of future vulnerability. A major product of this effort was to provide coping strategies for future expected changes. Both climate projections and response of vegetation were modeled (historical and GCM data for 2025-2034 and 2090-2099,VEMAP). Output from these efforts was used to inform workshops that were conducted to identify additional issues (socioeconomic), potential vulnerabilities, and coping strategies. This report is the second of a larger effort to assess future impacts and focused on agriculture, ranching/livestock systems, conservation, and natural areas and water (Appendix 2). From these efforts, Ojima and Lackett (2002) identified areas of greatest change.

Their analysis shows that the greatest increases in winter temperature are expected along the western parts of the Great Plains, especially along the Front Range. They also identified elements that will experience the greatest impact. For instance, winter moisture will favor cool season invasive species, woody perennials, and sagebrush; will reduce shallow aquifer recharge; will change streamflow timing; and will have consequences for forage availability and quality and disease incidence. Warmer winters will affect pest outbreaks, soil organic matter, community composition, grass, and exotic invasions (leafy spurge and Japanese brome may move south). Summer temperature increases are likely to impact hail, the spread of invasive tree species, and fire. From the social perspective, farm/ranch families will experience modified vulnerability as a result of climate impacts to ecological and market systems. Water use competition will change and will affect human residence as well as natural resource management.

Archer and Predick (2008) reviewed issues affecting SW habitats to identify impacts of expected climate change for plant and wildlife species. They based their analysis on a logical progression of expected outcomes for increases in temperature and changes to habitats and hydrological regimes within the SW. For instance, water availability will become more limited and riparian areas will shrink resulting in a decline of native fish species. They also expected a decrease in net primary productivity to lead to decreased carbon storage and increases in erosion and nonnative species. Ultimately, they predicted upward elevational shifts in plant communities and conditions, which increase mortality for dominant woody vegetation and open the door for greater establishment of nonnative annual grasses. Saguaros are expected to decline but increasing CO_2 may promote Joshua tree seedling survival leading to a shift in species dominance rather than loss of species. However, increased fires pose a major threat to this region's plant species. The impact of interactions of climate with non-climate stressors was emphasized in this study and, in particular, the authors noted that fire management will be a priority, particularly in shrublands, woodlands, and areas invaded by nonnative plants and exposed to increasing urbanization. Livestock enterprises may also be challenged on many fronts: reduced forage, forage quality, and more physiological stress reduces summer weight gains (high temps) and potentially increases disease.

5.4 Future Assessment Needs

The SW United States is biologically diverse, mirroring the diversity of habitats and microclimates present within this region. There is a clear need for more assessments that address many of the unique and at-risk habitats within this region. Animal species were almost exclusively assessed with index based methods, which though useful, often lack spatially relevant data that could be used to prioritize areas for management actions. Species level analyses for the SW need more efforts that incorporate distribution modeling and site specific studies. In addition, most animal species assessed were rare or special status, which limits application to broader assessments of natural communities or ecosystems. Only one assessment addressed fish (Furniss and others 2012) and none addressed invertebrates (though see Appendix 2 for some studies). Plants were typically assessed with niche model analyses and in particular BCE analysis. These approaches have different target scales, which leaves gaps in our knowledge for many species and habitats. Future assessments that address multiple scales and combine several methods for measuring vulnerability would create a more balanced understanding of future conditions and greater translatability of data to solutions for resource managers. We also noticed some inequality in the target area of the assessments conducted to date. No species-level assessments addressed areas in Northern New Mexico and northern Arizona. Data for this region could only be derived from larger-scale analyses. In addition, most modeling efforts have been conducted for tree species. More assessments are needed that focus on native grasslands and, in particular, incorporate recent findings with respect to invasive grassland species. We also identify new potential focus areas for future assessment work. Many studies of grassland and rangeland systems note the potential for change in forage quality through changes in both plant species composition and quality. However, we do not currently have any assessments that explore these relationships under climate change. Impacts from larger-scale analyses appear to identify greater vulnerability in transitional habitats. There is a need for more research and assessment of the importance of the types of habitats or transient habitat dynamics for ecosystem function and species conservation.

Many estimates for future climate fall outside of observed extreme events (e.g., Currie 2006). For species in the hot dry climates of the semiarid and arid SW that are already near their physiological limits, small changes in climate variables may have a disproportionate effect on population status and overall species composition (Enquist and Gori 2008; Enquist and others 2008). Measures of vulnerability that examine response experimentally or using process-based models may provide better information for an extreme future than bioclimate models or response based on past observations. Future studies and assessments need to incorporate physiological limitations to better model impacts. There is also a general need to explore thresholds of ecological change for many of these species and systems.

We also did not find studies that integrate the indirect and direct effects of climate change in an effective manner. For terrestrial systems, little work has focused on the influence of pathogens and pests. However, Dale and others (2001) and McPherson and Weltzin (2000) (Appendix 1) considered the effects of pest and disease in their reviews of climate change issues. Many modeling procedures used for habitat and larger-scale analyses in the SW are not adequate for estimating future species response because they do not consider dispersal, species interactions, and extreme events. McKenney and others (2007) incorporated dispersal considerations albeit in a somewhat limited manner, but none considered competitive interactions. This is a particularly important topic given recent findings that indicate a growing issue for invasive grass species (Bradley 2009). Better regional models of climate change, multiscale models linking climate variability and ecological processes, and integrated assessment of the potential impacts will allow managers and conservationist to provide viable response options for alternative climate futures.

Similar gaps were noted for assessments of water resources. Greater emphasis on assessments of terrestrial-aquatic linkages (Meyers and others 1999) is needed since many of the predicted changes to aquatic systems are mediated by surrounding terrestrial landscape (nutrient load, silt, etc.). Meyers and others (1999) noted that future information needs include more extensive datasets and better models to link hydrologic regime with various ecosystem processes and interactions. In particular, Meyers and others (1999) suggested vegetation composition and hydrology within the riparian zones as critical targets. This sentiment is echoed in the Environmental Protection Agency's report that considers climate change effects for three riparian systems in the United States (Julius and others 2006) as well as previous assessments of National Water Resources (Gleick and Adams 2000).

5.5 Using Assessments to Develop Adaptive Management Strategies for the Southwest

Vulnerability assessments are needed to better integrate climate change into current and future management plans. Through the assessment process, managers and researchers are able to pinpoint where and how species and habitats are likely to be influenced by global changes. Many current management practices, including restoration, reintroductions, and habitat preservation are based on the assumption that climatic variables will remain relatively stable. Climate change vulnerability assessments allow us to test this assumption and develop contingency plans where dramatic change is likely.

With increased knowledge, managers will also need more flexible planning strategies to allow them to focus on economically feasible actions (Chambers and Pellant 2008; Morgan and others 2008). This type of planning is likely to be better achieved through focus on output that identifies areas of greatest risk and recovery potential rather than on historic practices and knowledge (e.g., as is generated by state and transition models). This is especially true for the water sector where climate change is likely to result in widespread and irreversible changes to water availability and quality (Hurd and Coonrod 2003). Glick and others (2011) noted that future water management strategies will need to focus on the promotion of water conservation through protection and restoration of riparian areas and shifts in human land use practices. In addition, managers will increasingly need to consider the vulnerability not only of natural systems but of human systems. Turner and others (2003) detailed a framework for integrating environmental and human systems into traditional assessment processes.

Within the Forest Service, adaptive actions focus in the traditional areas of promoting ecosystem or habitat resilience and resistance under climate change as well as facilitating transition (FS Guide to Climate Change Scorecard; Peterson and others 2011). Climate change vulnerability assessments provide valuable information for managers who must determine the appropriate strategy for their natural resources. From the information generated by assessments of potential climate impacts and sensitivities, managers develop adaptation strategies (Fig. 1.1). Ultimately, managers must decide whether they are aiming to implement short-term stop gap measures to prevent damage and improve ecosystem resilience, or to plan for inevitable long-term changes. Where resources are available and highly desirable resources are at risk, short-term measures to improve resilience and resistance are warranted and desirable. In these situations, management activities will focus on preserving and restoring current communities and promoting resilience to disturbance. These activities may include promoting genetic adaptation, minimizing the impact of other stressors such as drought or reducing the likelihood of catastrophic disturbance (Williams and others 2010). Vulnerability assessments can be used to achieve these goals by identifying targets that are the least vulnerable to future changes (refugia in the sense of Gonzales and others 2010) or most able to adapt to new conditions. Vulnerability assessments provide a mechanism for identifying priorities both within and across a landscape by identifying areas of sensitivity and importance (see Gonzales and others 2010 for discussion). For example, vegetation models can identify areas at risk of invasions by exotic species (e.g., Aldridge 2008) or native invasive species (e.g., Zavaleta and Royval 2002); species-level assessments can point to additional climate related stresses for species already of conservation concern; and assessments can highlight opportunities to mitigate climate related impacts (e.g., Coe and others 2012; Bagne and others 2012). In the long-term, goals include strategies that focus more on sustaining ecosystem services such as clean air or water rather than conserving specific species or assemblages. This approach may become increasingly important as research points to the likely transition of many SW forest and habitats to new habitats under the combined pressures of climate and anthropogenic change. Management activities focused on assisting transition to a new state and potentially preserving some areas or communities that are expected to be reestablished elsewhere are examples of long-term approaches (Hansen and others 2001; Suttle and Thomsen 2007). Specific examples include replanting with drought-tolerant species, accelerating natural migration or dispersal of warm tolerant species, and transplanting schemes that use plants rather than seeds (Suttle and Thomsen 2007). Vulnerability assessments may also help form restoration strategies for areas most at risk of exceeding historic measures of variability and or be applied in analysis to determine the relative importance of lands for corridor preservation. The individual needs and interests of managers will determine the use of the information presented here. Climate change assessments are not meant to stand alone as a measure of future conditions but are meant to add to the body of knowledge on future threats and the sensitivity and strengths of individual components within the ecosystem. However, by nature, assessments are a valuable tool for identifying potential management intervention points. We hope that managers will use this report to locate potentially useful sources of information that are relevant to their own management plans.

5.6 Additional Information

The body of climate change literature and related assessment work is growing at an ever increasing rate from a diversity of disciplines. Within these assessments, there is considerable knowledge regarding potential climate change effects and we continue to improve the link between this knowledge of climate related impacts and decision-making processes (NCA 2011; Peterson and others 2011). The assessment process has its greatest value when it effectively evaluates potential responses to climate change and leads to improved planning efforts. Integration of climate change data is the first step toward developing effective adaptation options (Peterson and others 2011). However, variation in assessment methodologies and objectives creates challenges for managers and researchers who need information that both synthesizes data and provides comprehensive data on the vulnerability of biological systems and components.

The Forest Service Resources Planning Act assessment contains a number of chapters relating to climate change and synthesizes a great amount of literature regarding this topic (Joyce and Birdsey 2000). The USDA Forest Service Climate Change Science Center (http://www.fs.fed.us/ccrc/) is a repository of data, research, and tools for managing natural resources under a changing climate. In addition, many assessments are routinely conducted by the Forest Service at Unit, State, and Regional levels (e.g., Furniss and others 2012; various presented at http://www.fs.fed.us/ccrc/). Multiagency efforts are also generated in the form of Bureau of Land Management rapid ecological assessments. A series of resource based articles are available from Volume 21 of Climate Research (http://www.int-res.com/abstracts/cr/v21/n3/), which focuses on climate effects in the SW. This journal contains several articles that review current and forecasted weather and hydrology for the region and includes vulnerability analyses for social issues such as urban water use and ranching (Ojima and others 2002).

Accessibility is an important requirement for the successful integration of vulnerability assessments into management plans. Products such as Scanning the Conservation Horizons, which reviews vulnerability assessment methods and provides several working examples, are integral to improving the utility of information derived from these efforts (Glick and others 2011). A recent effort by the United States National Climate Assessment report (2011) developed guidelines and standards to structure the 2013 National Climate Vulnerability Assessment (NCA 2011) and the resulting framework has applications beyond that of the NCA. Several publications, including this synthesis, are designed to bridge the science-management gap (e.g., Peterson and others 2011). Peterson and others (2011) provided a toolkit for applying adaptation options to a variety of situations.

Finally, interagency collaborations and working groups play an increasingly important role in the dissemination of climate science information. Many of these programs and organizations have demonstrated successful strategies for organizing science and management across diverse user and stakeholder groups. The Malpai Borderlands Group and United Nations Educational, Scientific, and Cultural Organization biosphere reserve program, are examples of collaborations among Federal, state, tribal, and private groups to conserve SW ecosystems. These organizations are often able to reach goals together that might be more difficult than when approached on their own. The Sustainable Rivers Project collaboration between the Nature Conservancy and the U.S. Army Corps of Engineers aims to marry river conservation and dam management (Theobald and others 2005). The Southwestern Climate Change Initiative brings together non-profit, tribal, state, and Federal organizations to generate research that identifies ongoing and future issues relating to climate change in the SW. The Department of the Interior has established several regional Climate Science Centers (CSCs) to improve coordinated research efforts to better address the needs of land management agencies. A primary goal of this organization is to improved forecasts of conditions as well as the assessment of climate change vulnerability, risks and uncertainties. Federal programs such as the recently implemented CSCs and the Landscape Conservation Cooperatives (LCC) aim to support development of research programs and tools that deal with ongoing management issues. The Southcentral and Southwestern CSCs are organizing science needs and research for the SW, and the Desert and Southern Rockies LCCs are coordinating the development of tools and science delivery to managers within this region.

Literature Cited

Aldridge, C.L., [and others]. 2008. Region-wide Patterns of Greater Sage-Grouse Persistence. Diversity and Distributions 14: 983-994.

Allen Consulting Group. 2005. Climate Change Risk and Vulnerability: Promoting an Efficient Adaptation Response in Australia. Canberra, ACT: Australian Greenhouse Office, Department of the Environment and Heritage.

Archer, S., D.S. Schimel, and E.A. Holland. 2004. Mechanisms of Shrubland Expansion: Land Use, Climate, or CO_2? Climatic Change 29: 91-99.

Austin, D., P. Barabe, N. Benequista, A. Fish, [and others]. 2000. An assessment of climate vulnerability in the Middle San Pedro River. P. Finan, (ed.) T.J. West (ed.) Institute for the Study of Planet Earth, The University of Arizona Tucson, AZCLIMAS Report Series CL3-00.

Bachelet, D., J.M. Lenihan, C. Daly, R.P. Neilson, D.S. Ojima, and W.J. Parton. 2001a. MC1: A dynamic vegetation model for estimating the distribution of vegetation and associated ecosystem fluxes of carbon, nutrients and water. Department of Agriculture, Forest Service, Pacific Northwest Research Station. Gen. Tech. Rep. PNW-GTR-508: 1-95.

Bachelet, D., R.P. Neilson, J.M. Lenihan, and R.J. Drapek. 2001b. Climate change effects on vegetation distribution and carbon budget in the United States. Ecosystems 4:164-185.

Bagne, K.E., M.M. Friggens, and D.M. Finch. 2011. A System for Assessing Vulnerability of Species (SAVS) to Climate Change. Gen. Tech. Rep. RMRS-GTR-257. Fort Collins, CO. U.S. Department of Agriculture, Forest Service, Rocky Mountain Research Station. 28 p.

Bagne, K. E., and D. M. Finch. 2012. An assessment of vulnerability of threatened, endangered, and at-risk species to climate change at Fort Huachuca, Arizona. Gen. Tech. Rep. RMRS-GTR-284. Fort Collins, CO. U.S. Department of Agriculture, Forest Service, Rocky Mountain Research Station. 139 p.

Bagne, K. E., and D. Finch. 2013. Vulnerability of species to climate change in the Southwest: threatened, endangered, and at-risk species at Fort Huachuca, Arizona. Gen. Tech. Rep. RMRS-GTR-302. Fort Collins, CO: U.S. Department of Agriculture, Forest Service, Rocky Mountain Research Station. 183 p.

Bale, J. S., G. J. Masters, I. D. Hodkinson, [and others]. 2002. Herbivory in global climate change research: direct effects of rising temperature on insect herbivores. Malcolm C. Press, Ilias Symrnioudis, Allan.

Barron-Gafford, G., R. Scott, G.D. Jenerette, E.P. Hamerlynck, and T.E. Huxman. 2012. Temperature and precipitation controls over leaf- and ecosystem-level CO_2 flux along a woody plant encroachment gradient. Global Change Biology 18: 1389-1400.

Biringer, J. 2003. Forest Ecosystems Threatened by Climate Change: Promoting Long-term Forest Resilience. In: Hansen, L., Biringer, J.L., and Hoffman, J.R. (eds.) Buying Time: A User's A New Era for Conservation: Review of Climate Change Adaptation Literature March 12, 2009. 55 p.

Bradley, B.A. 2009. Regional analysis of the impacts of climate change on cheatgrass invasion shows potential risk and opportunity. Global Change Biology15: 196-208

Brennan, E.J. 2008. Reducing the Impact of Global Warming on Wildlife: The Science, Management, and Policy Challenges Ahead. Washington, DC: Defenders of Wildlife.

Breshears, D.D., [and others]. 2005. Regional Vegetation Die-off in Response to Global-change-type Drought. Proceedings of the National Academy of Sciences 102: 15144-15148.

Buckley, L.B. 2008. Linking traits to energetics and population dynamics to predict lizard ranges in changing environments. The American Naturalist 171: E1-E19.

Burkett, V.R., D.A. Wilcox, R. Stottlemyer, [and others]. 2005. Nonlinear dynamics in ecosystem response to climatic change: case studies and policy implications. Ecological Complexity 2: 357-394.

Chambers, J.C., and M. Pellant. 2008. Climate Change Impacts on Northwestern and Intermountain United States Rangelands. Wheat Ridge, CO: Society for Range Management.

Christensen, N.S., and D.P. Lettenmaier. 2007. A multimodal ensemble approach to assessment of climate change impacts on the hydrology and water resources of the Colorado River Basin, Hydrology and Earth System Sciences 11: 1417-1434. doi:10.5194/hess-11-1417-2007.

Climate Change Science Program [CCSP]. 2008b. The Effects of Climate Change on Agriculture, Land Resources, Water Resources, and Biodiversity in the United States. In: Buckland, P., Janetos, A. and Schimel, D., Synthesis and Assessment Product 4.3 Report by the U.S. Climate Change Science Program and the Subcommittee on Global Change Research. Washington, DC: U.S. Department of Agriculture 362 p.

Coe, S., D.M. Finch, and M.M. Friggens. 2012. An assessment of climate change and the vulnerability of wildlife in the Sky Islands of the Southwest. Gen. Tech. Rep. RMRS-GTR-273. Fort Collins, CO: U.S. Department of Agriculture, Forest Service, Rocky Mountain Research Station. 208 p.

Comer, P.J, B. Young, G. Schulz, [and others]. 2012. Climate Change Vulnerability and Adaptation Strategies for Natural Communities: Piloting Methods in the Mojave and Sonoran Deserts. Report to the U.S. Fish and Wildlife Service. NatureServe, Arlington, VA.

Currie, D. J. 2001. Projected effects of climate change on patterns of vertebrate and tree species richness in the conterminous United States. Ecosystems 4: 216-225.

Currie, D. J. 2001. Projected effects of climate change on patterns of vertebrate and tree species richness in the conterminous United States. Ecosystems 4: 216-225

Dale, V.H., L.A. Joyce, S. McNulty, [and others]. 2001. Climate change and forest disturbances. BioScience 51:723-734.

Daly, C., R.P. Neilson, and D.L. Phillips. 1994. A statistical topographic model for mapping climatological precipitation over mountainous terrain. Journal of Applied Meteorology 33: 140-158.

Daly, C., D. Bachelet, J.M. Lenihan, W. Parton, R.P. Neilson, and D. Ojima. 2000. Dynamic simulation of tree-grass interactions for global change studies. Ecological Applications 10(2): 449-469.

Diffenbaugh, N.S., F. Giorgi, and J.S. Pal. 2008. Climate change hotspots in the United States. Geophysical Research Letters 35: L16709, doi:10.1029/2008GL035075.

Dukes, J.S. 2002. Species Composition and Diversity Affect Grassland Susceptibility and Response to Invasion. Ecological Applications 12: 602-617.

Eaton, J.G. and R. M. Scheller. 1996. Effects of climate warming on fish thermal habitat in streams of the United States. Limnology Oceanography 41: 1109-1115.

Enquist, C., and D. Gori 2008a. Implications of Recent Climate Change and Conservation Priorities in New Mexico. The Nature Conservancy New Mexico Conservation Science Program, 79 p. Available at: http://www.nmconservation.org.

Enquist, C.F., E.H. Girvetz, and D.F. Gori. 2008b. A climate change vulnerability assessment for biodiversity in New Mexico, part II: Conservation implications of emerging moisture stress due to recent climate changes in New Mexico. Technical Report for Climate change ecology and adaptation program, The Nature Conservancy in New Mexico. 32 p.

Flather, C.H., M.S. Knowles, and J. McNees, 2008. Geographic patterns of at-risk species: A technical document supporting the USDA Forest Service Interim Update of the 2000 RPA Assessment. Gen. Tech. Rep. RMRS-GTR-211. Fort Collins, CO: U.S. Department of Agriculture, Forest Service, Rocky Mountain Research Station. 21 p.

Foden, W., G. Mace, J.-C. Vié, [and others]. 2008. Species susceptibility to climate change impacts. In: J.-C. Vié, C. Hilton-Taylor and S.N. Stuart (eds). The 2008 Review of The IUCN Red List of Threatened Species. IUCN Gland, Switzerland.

Fuhlendorf, S.D., and D.M. Engle. 2001. Restoring Heterogeneity on Rangelands: Ecosystem Management Based on Evolutionary Grazing Patterns. BioScience 51: 625-632.

Furniss, M. J., K.B. Roby, D. Cenderelli, [and others]. 2012. Assessing the Vulnerability of Watersheds to Climate Change: Results of National Forest Watershed Vulnerability Pilot Assessments. Climate Change Resource Center. U.S. Department of Agriculture, Forest Service. 305 p.

Galbraith, H., M.D. Dixon, J.C. Stromberg, and J.T. Price. 2010. Predicting climate change risks to riparian ecosystems in arid watersheds: the Upper San Pedro as a case study. In: Environmental Risk and Management from a Landscape Perspective. L.A. Kapustka and W.G. Landis, eds. John Wiley & Sons.

Gelbard, J.L. 2003. Grasslands at a Crossroads: Protecting and Enhancing Resilience to Climate Change. In: Hansen, L., Biringer, J.L., and Hoffman, J.R. (eds.) Buying Time: A User's Manual for Building Resistance and Resilience to Climate Change in Natural Systems (Berlin, Germany: World Wildlife Fund).

Glick, P., D. Inkley, and C. Tufts. 2001. Climate Change and Wildlife: Integrating Global Climate Policy Implementation with Local Conservation Action. Transactions of the 66th North American Wildlife and Natural Resources Conference. Washington, DC: Wildlife Management Institute.

Glick, P. 2005. Fish Out of Water: A Guide to Global Warming and Pacific Northwest Rivers Seattle, WA: National Wildlife Federation.

Glick, P., and J. Martin. 2008. A Great Wave Rising: Solutions for Columbia and Snake River Salmon in the Age of Global Warming. Seattle, WA: Light in the River.

Glick, P., J. Clough, and B. Nunley. 2008. Sea-Level Rise and Coastal Habitats in the Chesapeake Bay Region–Technical Report. Reston, VA: National Wildlife Federation.

Glick, P., A. Stuadt, and B. Stein. 2009. A new era for conservation; Review of climate change adaptation literature. National Wildlife Federation.

Gonzalez, P., R. P. Neilson, J. M. Lenihan, R. and J. Drapek. 2010. Global patterns in the vulnerability of ecosystems to vegetation shifts due to climate change. Global Ecology and Biogeography 19: 755–768.

Guisan, A., and R. Carsten. 2011. SESAM–a new framework integrating macroecological and species distribution models for predicting spatio-temporal patterns of species assemblages. Journal of Biogeography 38: 8.

Hamilton, D. 2008. Climate Change and the Challenges of Restoring Process-Driven Great Plains Grasslands. Presentation to the Western Stewardship Summit: Restoring Community and the Land, September 24-26, 2008, Sunriver, Oregon.

Hansen, A. J., R. P. Neilson, V. H. Dale, [and others]. 2001. Global Change in Forests: Responses of Species, Communities, and Biomes: Interactions between climate change and land use are projected to cause large shifts in biodiversity. BioScience 51: 765-779.

Hansen, L.J., J.L. Binger, and J.R. Hoffman (eds). 2003. Buying Time: Manual for Building Resistance and Resilience to Climate Change in Natural Systems. Berlin, Germany: World Wildlife Fund Climate Change Program. 246 p.

Hauer, F.R., J.S. Baron, D.H. Campbell, [and others]. 1997. Assessment of climate change and freshwater ecosystems of the Rocky Mountains, USA and Canada. Hydrological Processes 11: 903-924.

Herrick, J., Balnap, J., Bestelmeyer, B.T.,[and others]. 2004. Experimental Definition of Resilience for State-and-Transition Models. Proceedings 57th Annual Meeting for the Society of Range Management. Salt Lake City, UT, January 24-30.

Hunt, H.W., M.J. Trilica, E.F. Frenete, [and others]. 1991. Simulation model for the effects of climate change on temperate grassland ecosystems. Ecological Modeling 53: 205-246.

Hurd, B.H., and J. Coonrod. 2008. Climate Change and its implications for New Mexico's Water resources and economic opportunities. New Mexico State University Technical Report 45. 28 p.

Hurtt, G.C., S.W. Pacala, P.R. Moorcroft, [and others]. 2002. Projecting the future of the U.S. carbon sink. Proceedings of the National Academy of Sciences 99: 1389-1394

Inkley, D.B., [and others]. 2004. Global Climate Change and Wildlife in North America. Bethesda, MD: The Wildlife Society.

Jiguet, F.. 2006. Thermal range predicts bird population resilience to extreme high temperatures. Ecology Letters 9: 1321-30.

Johnson, W.C., B.V. Millett, T. Gilmanov, R.A. [and others]. 2005. Vulnerability of northern prairie wetlands to climate change. BioScience 55: 863-872.

Joyce, L.A., and R. Birdsey (tech eds.). 2000. The impact of climate change on America's forests: a technical document supporting the 2000 USDA forest service RPA assessment. Gen. Tech. Rep. RMRS-GTR-59. Fort Collins, CO: U.S. Department of Agriculture, Forest Service, Rocky Mountain Research Station. 133 p.

Joyce, L., [and others]. 2001. Potential Consequences of Climate Variability and Change for the Forests of the United States. Chapter 17. Climate Change Impacts on the United States: The Potential Consequences of Climate Variability and Change, Report by the National Assessment Synthesis Team. Cambridge, U.K.: Cambridge University Press: 489-522.

Joyce, L.A., [and others]. 2008. National Forests. Chapter 3 in S.H. Julius and J.M. West (eds.) Preliminary Review of Adaptation Options for Climate-Sensitive Ecosystems and Resources. A Report by the U.S. Climate Change Science Program and the Subcommittee on Global Change Research. Washington, DC: 3-1 to 3-127.

Joyce, L.A., C.H. Flather, and M. Koopman. 2008. WHPRP Final Project Report: 1.B: Analysis of Potential Impacts of Climate Change on Wildlife Habitats in the U.S. Available at: http://www.tribesandclimatechange.org/docs/tribes_214.pdf

Kearney, M., W.P. Porter, C. Williams, S. Ritchie, and A. Hoffmann. 2009. Integrating biophysical models and evolutionary theory to predict climatic impacts on species' ranges: the dengue mosquito *Aedes aegypti* in Australia. Functional Ecology 23: 528-538.

Klopfenstein, N.B., M.-S. Kim, J.W. Hanna, B.A. Richardson, and J. Lundquist. 2009. Approaches to predicting potential impacts of climate change on forest disease: An example with Armillaria root disease. USDA Forest Service. Res. Pap. RMRS-RP-76.

Kranjcec, J., F.M. Mahoney, and S.B. Rood. 1998. The responses of three riparian cottonwood species to water table declines. Forest Ecology and Management 110: 77-87.

Kupfer, J.A, J. Balmat, and J.L. Smith. 2005. Shifts in the potential distribution of Sky Island plant communities in response to climate change. USDA Forest Service. Proc. RMRS-P-36.

Lawler, J.J., S.L. Shafer, B.A. Bancroft, and A.R. Blaustein. 2010. Projected Climate Impacts for the Amphibians of the Western Hemisphere. Conservation Biology 24:1, 38-50.

Lawler, J. J., S. L. Shafer, D. White, [and others]. 2009. Projected climate-induced faunal change in the Western Hemisphere. Ecology 90: 588-597.

McCabe, G.J., and D.M. Wolock. 1999. General Circulation Model Simulations of Future Snowpack in the Western United States. Journal of the American Water Resources Association 35: 1473-1484.

McKenney, D. W., Pedlar, J. H., Lawrence, K., Campbell, K., and M. F. Hutchinson. 2007. Potential impacts of climate change on the distribution of North American trees. Bioscience 57: 939-948.

Meyer, J. L., Sale, M. J., Mulholland, P. J., & Poff, N. L. 1999. Impacts of climate change on aquatic ecosystem functioning and health. Journal of the American Water Resources Association 35: 1373-1386.

Mitchell, C.E., D. Tilman, and J.V. Groth. 2002. Effects of Grassland Plant Species Diversity, Abundance, and Composition on Foliar Fungal Disease. Ecology 83: 1713-1726.

Mokany, K., and S. Ferrier. 2011. Predicting impacts of climate change on biodiversity: a role for semi-mechanistic community-level modeling. Diversity and Distributions 17: 2.

Morgan, J.A., J.D. Derner, D.G. Milchunas, and E. Pendall. 2008. 57th Annual Meeting, Society for Range Management, Abstract No. 142. Management Implications of Global Change for Great Plains Rangelands. Wheat Ridge, CO: Society for Range Management. June 2008, Vol. 30: 18-22.

Neilson, R.P., I.C. Prentice, B. Smith, T.G.F. Kittel, and D. Viner.1998. Simulated changes in vegetation distribution under global warming. In: The Regional Impacts of Climate Change: An Assessment of Vulnerability. R.T. Watson, M.C. Zinyowera, R.H. Moss, and D.J. Dokken (eds.) Cambridge University Press, Cambridge: 439-456.

New Mexico Department of Game and Fish [NMDGF]. 2006. Comprehensive Wildlife Conservation Strategy for New Mexico. Technical Report, New Mexico Department of Game and Fish, New Mexico Cooperative Fish and Wildlife Research Unit. Santa Fe, New Mexico. 526 p. + appendices. Available at: http://fws-case10.nmsu.edu/cwcs/sortspatialdata.php.

Notaro, M., Mauss, A., and J.W. Williams. 2012. Projected vegetation changes for the American Southwest: combined dynamic modeling and bioclimatic-envelope approach. Ecological Applications 22: 1365-1388.

Ojima, D.S., and J.M. Lackett, (comps). 2000. National Assessment Synthesis Team. Climate Change Impacts on the United States: The Potential Consequences of Climate Variability and Change. Report for the Global Change Research Program. New York: Cambridge University Press.

Ojima, D.S., and J.M. Lackett, and the Central Great Plains Steering Committee and Assessment Team. 2002. Preparing for a Changing Climate: The Potential Consequences of Climate Variability and Change–Central Great Plains. Report for the U.S. Global Change Research Program. Colorado State University. 103 p.

Patrick, L.D., K. Ogle, C.W. Bell, J. Zak, D. Tissue. 2009. Physiological responses of two contrasting desert plant species to precipitation variability are differentially regulated by soil moisture and nitrogen dynamics. Global Change Biology 15: 1214-1229.

Peery, M.Z., R.J. Gutièrrez, R. Kirby, O.E. Ledee, and W. Lahaye. 2012. Climate change and spotted owls: potentially contrasting responses in the Southwestern U.S. Global Change Biology 18: 865-880.

Peters, D.P.C., R.A. Pielke, B.T. Bestelmeyer, [and others]. 2004. Cross-scale interactions, nonlinearities, and forecasting catastrophic events. Proceedings of the National Academy of Sciences (USA) 101: 15130-15135.

Peterson, D.L., C.I. Millar, L.A. Joyce, [and others]. 2011. Responding to climate change in National Forests: a guidebook for developing adaptation options. Gen. Tech. Rep. PNW-GTR-855. Portland, OR: U.S. Department of Agriculture, Forest Service, Pacific Northwest Research Station. 109 p.

Peterson, G.D., G.S. Cumming, and S.R. Carpenter. 2003. Scenario Planning: A Tool for Conservation in an Uncertain World. Conservation Biology 17: 358-366.

Pierce, D.W., [and others]. 2008. Attribution of Declining Western U.S. Snowpack to Human Effects. Journal of Climate 21: 6425-6444.

Poiani, K.A., W.C. Johnson, G.A. Swanson, and T.C. Winter. 1996. Climate change and northern prairie wetlands: Simulations of long-term dynamics. Limnology and Oceanography 41: 871-881.

Rehfeldt, G.E., N.L. Crookston, M.V. Warwell, and J.S. Evans. 2006. Empirical analyses of plant-climate relationships for the western United States. International Journal of Plant Science 167:1123-1150.

Root, T.L., and S.H. Schneider. 2002. Climate Change: Overview and Implications for Wildlife. In: Schneider and Root (eds.) Wildlife Responses to Climate Change: North American Case Studies. Washington, DC: Island Press.

Rowland, E.L., J.E. Davison, and L.J. Graumlich. 2011. Approaches to Evaluating Climate Change Impacts on Species: A Guide to Initiating the Adaptation Planning Process. Environmental Management 47(3): 322-337.

Ryan, M., S. Archer, R. Birdsey, [and others]. 2008. Land Resources. In: The effects of climate change on agriculture, land resources, water resources, and biodiversity. A Report by the U.S. Climate Change Science Program and the Subcommittee on Global Change Research. Washington, DC. 362 p.

Schimel, D., J. Melillo, H. Tian, [and others]. 2000. Contribution of increasing CO_2 and climate to carbon storage by ecosystems in the United States. Science 287: 2004-2006.

Schloss, C.A., T.A. Nunez, and J.J. Lawler. 2012. Dispersal will limit ability of mammals to track climate change in the Western Hemisphere. Proceedings of the National Academy of Sciences 109: 8606-8611.

Seager, R., [and others]. 2007. Model Predictions of an Imminent Transition to a More Arid Climate in Southwestern North America. Science 316: 1181-1184.

Sekercioglu, C.H., S.H. Schneider, J.P. Fay, and S.R. Loarie. 2008. Climate change, elevation range shifts, and bird extinctions. Conservation Biology 22: 140-150.

Shafer, S.L., P.J. Bartlein, and R.S. Thompson. 2001. Potential changes in the distribution of western North America tree and shrub taxa under future climate scenarios. Ecosystems 4:200-215.

Sheppard, P.R., A.C. Comrie, [and others]. 2002. The climate of the US Southwest. Climate Research 21: 219-238.

Skirvin, S.M., S.E. Drake, M.P. McClaran, S.E. March, and D.M. Meko. 2000. Climate change and land tenure: potential impacts on vegetation and developments in the San Pedro River watershed, southeastern Arizona. 4th International Conference on Integrating GIS and Environmental Modeling: Problems, Prospects and Research Needs; Banff, Alberta, Canada; Sept 2-8.

Smith, S.D., T.E. Huxman, S.F. Zitzer, T.N.[and others]. 2000. Elevated CO_2 increases productivity and invasive species success in an arid ecosystem. Nature 408:79-82.

Steinke, R. 2012. Assessment of Watershed Vulnerability to Climate Change, Coconino National Forest. In: M. J. Furniss, Roby, K. B., Cenderelli, D., Chatel, J., Clifton, C. F., Clingenpeel, A., and others. Assessing the Vulnerability of Watersheds to Climate Change: Results of National Forest Watershed Vulnerability Pilot Assessments. Climate Change Resource Center. U.S. Department of Agriculture, Forest Service. 305 p.

Stewart, I.T., D.R. Cayan, and M.D. Detinger. 2004. Changes in snowmelt runoff timing in western North America under a "business as usual" climate change scenario. Climate Change 62: 217-232.

Stromberg, J. C. 2001. Restoration of riparian vegetation in the south-western United States: importance of flow regimes and fluvial dynamism. Journal of Arid Environments 49: 17-34.

Stromberg, J., M.D. Dixon, R.L. Scott, T. Maddock, K. Baird, and B. Tellman. 2009. Status of the Upper San Pedro River (United States) Riparian Ecosystem. In: Ecology and Conservation of the San Pedro River. Ed. by J. C. Stromberg and B. J. Tellman. Tucson: University of Arizona Press: 371-387.

Suttle, K.B., and M.A. Thomsen. 2007. Climate Change and Grassland Restoration in California: Lessons from Six Years of Rainfall Manipulation in a North Coast Grassland. Madroño 54: 225-233.

Theobald, D.M., D.M. Merritt, and J.B. Norman, III. 2010. Assessment of Threats to Riparian Ecosystems in the Western U.S. A report presented to The Western Environmental Threats Assessment Center, Priveville, OR: USDA Stream Systems Technology Center and Colorado State University, Fort Collins. 61 p.

Thomas, C.D., A. Cameron, R.E. Green, [and others]. 2004. Extinction risk from climate change. Nature 427: 145-148.

Thompson, R.S., S.W. Hostetler, P.J. Bartlein, and K.H. Anderson. 1998. A strategy for assessing potential future change in climate, hydrology, and vegetation in the western United States. USGS Circular 1153. U.S. Geological Survey, Washington, DC.

Turner, B.L., II, R.E. Kasperson, P. Matson, [and others]. 2003. A framework for vulnerability analysis in sustainability science. Proceedings of the National Academy of Sciences 100: 8074-8079.

U.S. Global Change Research Program [USGCRP]. 2011. The United States National Climate Assessment. Uses of Vulnerability Assessments for the National Climate Assessment. NCA Report Series, Volume 9. Washington, DC. Available at: http://www.globalchange.gov/images/NCA/NCA-Vulnerability-Assessments-Workshop-Report.pdf.

USDA Forest Service. 2011. Navigating the Climate Change Performance Scorecard. A Guide for National Forest and Grasslands, Version 2. Available at: http://www.fs.fed.us/climatechange/advisor/scorecard/scorecard-guidance-08-2011.pdf.

Van Mantgem, P.J., [and others]. 2009. Widespread Increase of Tree Mortality Rates in the Western United States. Science 323: 521-524.

Watt, D., and John B. Whittaker. 2002. Herbivory in global climate change research: direct effects of rising temperature on insect herbivores. Global Change Biology 8: 1-16.

Weiss, J.L., and J.T. Overpeck. 2005. Is the Sonoran desert losing its cool? Global Change Biology 11: 2065-2077.

Welling, L. 2008. Climate Change Scenario Planning: A Tool for Managing Resources in an Era of Uncertainty. Presentation to Mountain Climate 2008, 9-12 June, Silverton, CO. Sponsored by the Consortium for Integrated Climate Research in the Western Mountains.

Westerling, A.L., [and others]. 2006. Warming and Earlier Spring Increases Western U.S. Forest Wildfire Activity. Science 313: 940-943.

Wilcove, D.S., D. Rothstein, J. Dubow, A. Phillips, and E. Losos. 1998. Quantifying threats to imperiled species in the United States. BioScience 48: 607-615.

Williams, A.P., C.D. Allen, C.I. Millar, [and others]. 2010. Forest Responses to increasing aridity and warmth in the southwestern United States. Proceedings of the National Academy of Sciences 107: 21289-21294.

Williams, A.P., C.D. Allen, A.K. Macalady, [and others]. 2012. Temperature as a potent driver of regional forest drought stress and tree mortality. Nature Climate Change 1693: 1-6.

Wilson, R. and S. Turton. 2011. Climate change adaptation options, tools and vulnerability. Contribution of Work Package 4 to the Forest Vulnerability Assessment. Report. National Climate Change Adaptation Research Facility (NCCARF), Gold Coast, QLD, Australia.

Winter, T.C. 2000. The vulnerability of wetlands to climate change: A hydrologic landscape perspective. Journal of the American Water Resources Association 36: 305-311.

Young, J.A., and R.R. Blank. 1995. Cheatgrass and Wildfires in the Intermountain West. 1995 Symposium Proceedings. California Exotic Pest Plant Council, California. Available at: http://www.cal-ipc.org/symposia/archive/pdf/1995_symposium_proceedings1792.pdf

Young, B., Byers, E., Gravuer, [and others]. 2010. Guidelines for using the NatureServe climate change vulnerability index. NatureServe, Arlington, VA.

Zack, S., K. Ellison, M. Cross, and E. Rowland. 2010. Climate change planning for the Great Plains: Wildlife vulnerability assessment and recommendations for land and grazing management. Summary Report, Wildlife Conservation Society, North America Program.

Zavaleta, E.S., and J.L. Royval. 2002. Climate Change and the Susceptibility of U.S. Ecosystems to Biological Invasions: Two Cases of Expected Range Expansion. In: S.H. Schneider and T.L. Root (eds.), Wildlife Responses to Climate Change: North American Case Studies. Washington, DC: Island Press: 277-341.

Appendix 1. Examples of specific programs and analysis methods (see Box 3.1) for models used to estimate species distribution (environmental envelope, simulation models) or species adaptive capacity (adaptive capacity models) in climate change vulnerability assessments. This list is not comprehensive but gives representative examples of different methods employed and commonly used programs. Examples of methods used in projects are presented in Table 4.2.

Type	Examples	Analysis	Purpose	Target/ scope	Source
Adaptive Capacity Models					
	Landscape Resistance Models	Landscape analyses	Estimates cost per pixel of land cover type as it relates to species presence. Translates into dispersal ability of species under various scenarios. Species with the greatest limitations have the least adaptive capacity.	Species and ecosystems	Cushman and others 2006
	RAMAS	Viability analysis	Links geographic data (including land change data) to metapopulation models to generate population statistics.	Plant or animal populations	http://www.ramas.com/ramas.htm#gis
	MigClim: Simulating migration under climate change	Machine learning Method	Cellular Automaton model that simulates plant dispersal under climate change and landscape fragmentation scenarios. Used in conjunction with envelope type analysis (requires maps of current and future suitable habitat distributions).	Plants, user defined area	http://cran.r-project.org/web/packages/MigClim/index.html
Dynamic Bioenergetic/ Ecophysiological Models					
	Various	Varies (see text)	Typically an analysis that links a bioenergetic or biophysical model with models of species traits relative to species extinction under climate change. Can be used to estimate species distribution or persistence under climate change. Depending upon the output, this approach may produce an estimate of species distribution or adaptive capacity.	Animal and plant species	Used by Buckley 2008 for plants and animals and by Kearney and others 2009 for mosquitoes
Environmental Envelope Models					
	Genetic Algorithm for Rule-Set Prediction (GARP)	Machine learning method	Niche model; uses spatial data on temperature, rainfall, and elevation with point data on species range to estimate potential range	Native and non-native species	nhm.ku.edu/destopgarp
	Maximum entropy (Maxent)	Machine learning method	Habitat model; uses set of environmental variables and georeferenced occurrence (presence absence data) locations to produce models of species' ranges	Animal or plant species	http://www.cs.princeton.edu/~schapire/maxent/
	Statistical Species Distribution Models (SSDM)	Regression	Predicts potential distribution of species and colonization based on 7 climate and 31 site and soil variables.	Tree species, no temporal component	www.nrs.fs.fed.us/atlas
	SPECIES: Spatial Evaluation of Climate Impact on the Envelope of Species.	Machine learning method	Predict suitable habitat of species using neural network analyses	Species	Pearson and others 2002

Type	Examples	Analysis	Purpose	Target/scope	Source
Hydrological Models					
	Regional Hydro-Ecologic Simulation System (RHESSys)	Regression	GIS-based hydro-ecological model simulates water, carbon, and nutrient flow	Watershed	fiesta.bren.ucsb. edu/~rhessys/ setup/downloads/ downloads.html
	Sea Level Affecting Marshes Model (SLAMM)	Regression	Models processes dominating wetland conversion and shoreline modification	Coastal areas	http://www. slammview.org.
	Variable Infiltration Capacity		Physically based distributed hydrological model; suited for water/energy balance studies, so used extensively in climate change studies	River/stream/ reservoir systems	Christensen and Lettenmaier, 2007
	Dynamic Ecophysiological Models	Ecophysiological model	Models fish growth rates, algae production, and similar under various environmental conditions	Fish	Keith and others, 2008.
Simulation/Process-Based Models					
Biogeographic Models					
	BIOME, DOLY, MAPSS	Regression	Biogeographic equilibrium models that calculate plant available water and temperature thresholds according to climatic zone, life form, and plant type.	Vegetation types; area defined by user	www.fs.fed.us/ pnw/corvaliis/ mdr/mapss
Biogeochemical Models					
	Instantaneous Canopy Flux Model (PnET)	Regression	Biogeochemical model that merges three computational models that simulate carbon, water, and nitrogen dynamics	Forest ecosystems; typical scale = 5 km	http://www. pnet.sr.unh.edu/ download.html
	Soil Organic Matter Model (CENTURY)	Regression	Biogeochemical model that simulates nutrient/ hydrological flows and includes fire/harvest frequency on monthly scale	Watershed; typical scale = 5 km	www.nrel. colostate.edu/ project/century5/
	BIOCLIM (BIOMAP)	Regression	Prediction system (biogeochemical model) that uses mean monthly climate estimates to predict energy and water balances at specified location	Vegetation type; area defined by user	software. infromer.com/ getfree-bioclim-download-software
	DAYCENT	Simulation model	Biogeochemical model that simulates nutrient/ hydrological flows and includes fire/harvest frequency on a daily scale. Daily version of CENTURY.	Vegetation types; watershed; typical scale = 5km.	www.nrel. colostate.edu/ project/century5/
Dynamic Global Vegetation Model (DGVM)					
	LANDIS, LANDIS II	Simulation Model	Simulates dynamic interactions between vegetation, climate and disturbance. Can also incorporate dispersal as the probability of a seed moving to a new cell. Like other process based models, LANDIS can be used to develop projections of future distribution but does not in and of itself do so. LANDIS II relies on FIA data	Tree species age classes. Multiple scales though typically =10km.	http://www.fs.fed. us/pnw/mdr/ mapss

Type	Examples	Analysis	Purpose	Target/ scope	Source
	MC1	Regression	(DGVM) Combines biogeographic with biogeochemical models (CENTURY and MAPSS) and fire models to identify composition of plant groups under varying conditions.	Plant physiognomic group; Multiple scales typically 10km	http//www.fsl. orst.edu/dgvm
GAP models					
	FOREL, JABOWA, ZELIG, FORSKA	Simulation Model	Also known as succession models. Simulates gap dynamics and stand dynamics of forests by using individual based models that simulate interactions and dynamics. Typically applied to mixed species forests.	Individual and species level by patch	http://www.pik-potsdam.de/topik/ t6scs/safe/home/ forclim.html
Integrated Models					
	Tree Mig	Simulation Model	Forest dynamics are simulated with a multi-species, height structured forest model which considers growth, competition, death as well as seed productions, seed bank dynamics, germination, and sapling development under various environmental conditions.	Tree species	Lischke and others 2006
	The Terrestrial Observation and Prediction System (TOPS)	Simulation framework	Simulation framework. Links historical climate data, remotely sensed data, climate projections, and species response (via distribution analysis) models.	Plant species	Nemani and others 2009
	FireBGCv2	Simulation model	Simulation modeling platform. Links mechanistic vegetation succession model (a spatially explicit fire model incorporating ignition, spread, and effects on ecosystem components) and a detailed fuel treatment module. FireBGCv2 dynamically simulates synergistic and interacting effects of weather and climatology, vegetation growth and succession, disturbance (e.g., wildfire, bark beetles), and land management (e.g., prescribed fire, thinning) on landscape structure and ecosystem processes.	Plant type	Keane and others 2011; Loehman and others 2011

Appendix 2. Studies that present analysis, theoretical context, and/or background data for potential species' responses to future climate conditions, with an emphasis on literature relevant to the SW United States. "na" represent Not Applicable.

Author/Year	Title	Location	Target
Archer and others 2004	Tree and shrub encroachment is a result of combination of climate, CO_2, fire regimes, livestock grazing	U.S.	Trees and Shrubs
Audubon 2009	Birds and climate change: ecological disruption in motion	U.S.	Birds
Austin and others 2000	An assessment of climate vulnerability in the Middle San Pedro River	San Pedro River	Social
Bachelet and others 2001	Climate change effects on vegetation distribution and carbon budget in the United States	U.S.	Nutrients, NPP
Bale and others 2002	Herbivory in global climate change research: direct effects of rising temperature on insect herbivores	Global	Insect herbivores
Barron-Gaffin and others 2012	Temperature and precipitation controls over leaf- and ecosystem-level CO_2 flux along a woody plant encroachment gradient	Global	Plant functional type
Bowers 2007	Has climatic warming altered spring flowering date of Sonoran desert shrubs?	Sonoran Desert	Shrubs
Bradley 2010	Assessing ecosystem threats from global and regional change: hierarchical modeling of risk to sagebrush ecosystems from climate change, land use and invasive species in Nevada, USA	Nevada	Sagebrush habitat/ *Bromus tectorum*
Crimmins and others 2009	Flowering range changes across an elevation gradient in response to warmer summer temperatures	Arizona	Plants
Daly and others 2000	Dynamic simulation of tree-grass interactions for global change studies	South Dakota	Plants
Early and Sax 2011	Analysis of climate paths reveals potential limitations on species range shifts	Western U.S.	15 amphibians
Ehlringer and others 1991	Differential utilization of summer rains by desert plant	Utah	Plants
Eisen and others 2007	A spatial model of shared risk for plague and hantavirus pulmonary syndrome in the southwestern United States	Southwestern U.S.	Disease
Flather and others 2008	Geographic patterns of at-risk species	U.S.	T&E species
Goodrich and Ellis 2008	Climatic controls and hydrologic impacts of a recent extreme seasonal precipitation reversal in Arizona	Southwestern U.S.	Water
Graham and Nobel 1996	Long-term effects of a coupled atmospheric CO_2 concentration on the CAM species *Agave deserti*	Southwestern U.S.	Agave
Guarin and Taylor 2005	Drought triggered tree mortality in mixed conifer forests in Yosemite National Park, California, USA	California	Trees
Hunt and others 1991	Simulation model for the effects of climate change on temperate grassland ecosystems	U.S.	Shortgrass prairie
Hurtt and others 2002	Projecting the future of the U.S. carbon sink	U.S.	Carbon
Jiguet and others 2006	Thermal range predicts bird population resilience to extreme high temperatures	France	Birds
Johnson and others 2005	Vulnerability of northern prairie wetlands to climate change	Prairie pothole region	Waterfowl habitat
Kearney and others 2009	Integrating biophysical models and evolutionary theory	Australia	Mosquitoes
Klopfenstein and others 2009	Approaches to predicting potential impacts of climate change on forest disease: An example with armillaria root disease	Northwest U.S.	Armillaria root disease
Kranjcec and others 1998	The responses of three riparian cottonwood species to water table decline	Western U.S.	Cottonwood
McCabe and Wolock 1999	General-circulation-model simulations of future snowpack in the western United States	Southern Rockies	Water

Author/Year	Title	Location	Target
McDonald and Brown 1992	Using montane mammals to model extinctions due to global change	Western U.S.	Vegetation/mammals
Morgan and others 2011	Management Implications of global change for great plains rangelands	Western U.S.	Rangelands
Patrick and others 2009	Physiological responses of two contrasting desert plant species to precipitation variability are differentially regulated by soil moisture and nitrogen dynamics	Texas	Plants
Pierce and others 2008	Attribution of Declining Western U.S. Snowpack to Human Effects	Western U.S.	Water
Poiani and others 1996	Climate change and northern prairie wetlands: Simulations of long-term dynamics	Western U.S.	Habitats
Root 1988	Energy constraints on avian distribution and abundances	U.S.	Birds
Rowland and others 2011	Approaches to evaluating climate change impacts on species: A guide to initiating the adaptation planning process	na	Plants, animal, water
Schimel 2000	Contribution of increasing CO_2 and climate to carbon storage by ecosystems of the United States		Habitats
Seager and others 2007	Model projections of an imminent transition to a more arid climate in southwestern North America	Southwestern U.S.	Climate projections
Sekercioglu and others 2008	Climate change, elevation range shifts, and bird extinctions	Global	Birds
Sheppard and others 2002	The climate of the US Southwest	Southwestern U.S.	Climate projections
Skirvin and others 2000	Climate change and land tenure: potential impacts on vegetation and developments in the San Pedro River watershed, southwestern Arizona	Arizona	Plant species in Sand Pedro River
Smith and others 2000	Elevated CO_2 increases productivity and invasive species success in an arid ecosystem	Western U.S.	Cheatgrass
Stewart and others 2004	Changes in snowmelt runoff timing in western North America under a "business as usual" climate change scenario	Western U.S.	Water
Weiss and Overpeck 2005	Is the Sonoran desert losing its cool?	Southwestern U.S.	Climate projections
White and others 2009	Past and projected rural land conversion in the US at state, regional, and national levels	U.S. by region	Socio-economic Land use
Zavaleta and Royval 2002	Climate change and the susceptibility of U.S. ecosystems to biological invasions: Two cases of expected range expansion		
Schloss and others 2012	Dispersal will limit ability of mammals to track climate change in the Western Hemisphere	Western Hemisphere	Mammals
Shafer and others 2001	Potential changes in the distribution of western North America tree and shrub taxa under future climate scenarios	Western U.S.	Tree and shrub species
Williams and others 2012	Temperature as a potent driver of regional forest drought stress and tree mortality	na	Tree productivity and survival
Thompson and others 1998	A strategy for assessing potential future change in climate, hydrology, and vegetation in the western United States	Western U.S.	Vegetation and water
Rehfeldt and others 2006	Empirical analyses of plant-climate relationships for the western United States	Western U.S.	Plant biotic communities

Rocky Mountain Research Station

The Rocky Mountain Research Station develops scientific information and technology to improve management, protection, and use of the forests and rangelands. Research is designed to meet the needs of the National Forest managers, Federal and State agencies, public and private organizations, academic institutions, industry, and individuals. Studies accelerate solutions to problems involving ecosystems, range, forests, water, recreation, fire, resource inventory, land reclamation, community sustainability, forest engineering technology, multiple use economics, wildlife and fish habitat, and forest insects and diseases. Studies are conducted cooperatively, and applications may be found worldwide. For more information, please visit the RMRS web site at: www.fs.fed.us/rmrs.

Station Headquarters
Rocky Mountain Research Station
240 W Prospect Road
Fort Collins, CO 80526
(970) 498-1100

Research Locations

Flagstaff, Arizona	Reno, Nevada
Fort Collins, Colorado	Albuquerque, New Mexico
Boise, Idaho	Rapid City, South Dakota
Moscow, Idaho	Logan, Utah
Bozeman, Montana	Ogden, Utah
Missoula, Montana	Provo, Utah

To learn more about RMRS publications or search our online titles:

www.fs.fed.us/rm/publications

www.treesearch.fs.fed.us